David,

When I saw this book, I thought of you and decided to keep it for a special occasion. Well, tonight is a special occasion and someday you'll look back and know that it was.

You worked hard for this special honor and deserve it. But, David, don't stop now. Keep going and strive for bigger and better goals. Set your standards high, whether they be moral or material.

When reading these poems, think of me because when I read them, they're exactly what I would say to you as you grow into manhood.

I'm proud of you.

Love, Mom

(The inscription on the book of poems *Don't Ever Give Up Your Dreams* that my mother gave to me upon my high school graduation.)

JOURNEY
to JOY

A Boy Unveiled

DAVID TUTERA

Dada Media softcover edition 2022

Edited by Paula J Marchese

Design by David Tutera

Library of Congress Cataloguing-in-Publication Data

Names: Tutera, David, author

Title: Journey to Joy: A Boy Unveiled /David Tutera

Description: Softcover edition (2022)

Identifiers: LCCN 2022913274

Subjects: LCSH: Tutera, David. Coming of age. United States. Celebrity. LGBTQ. Memoir.

Classification:

ISBN: 978-1-66787-552-1

eBook ISBN: 978-1-66787-553-8

This book is dedicated to my mom, my husband Joey, and my daughters, Cielo and Gracie.

"A heart is shown not by how much you love, but by how much you are loved by others."

-*The Wizard of Oz*

CONTENTS

AUTHOR'S NOTE

Some of the events in this book took place more than thirty years ago. Some family members may have different recollections of our past. We all have our stories of life and this is my experience, what I felt, what I heard and what I saw. I have tried to recount the events in this book to the best of my own memories. Some people's names and identifying characteristics have been changed for privacy reasons. I have also had to compress some timelines for clarity of the storyline.

INTRODUCTION

November 2019, I was standing backstage at the largest Wedding conference in Las Vegas, getting ready to speak to an enthusiastic, welcoming audience—something I'd done numerous times before. Sitting out there were many faces I recognized as well as many I'd never met, all expectant and waiting for me. I absolutely love this part of my life, connecting with people and sharing my experiences and advice in hopes that they will be inspired to follow and capture their own big dreams.

But for the first time ever—and I mean ever—I was nervous. Palms sweating, heart racing, hesitating to walk out onto the stage—the whole nine yards. Then I heard my husband Joey's voice in my head: *"You can do this. It's time to share your story."*

Many people know that I started my event-planning business when I was around nineteen, in my home town of Port Chester, New York. And that I grew that business over the years to include books, television shows, and even my own line of wedding dresses, rings, and more. Besides my beautiful daughters and my life with Joey, nothing has made me happier than being able to help people make the most important day of their lives exactly as they envisioned it. Their celebrations have become a part of me.

I had big dreams when I was younger; I persevered and worked my ass off to make them a reality. But there's more. Much more. If not for Joey's love and encouragement, I know I would not have been standing offstage that day about to step out and share my *entire* story. And it terrified me and excited me all at the same time. In fact, the night before my appearance,

I actually wrote a "Plan B" speech, just in case I truly lost my nerve. Thankfully, I didn't. I knew in my heart that opening up my life in this way would not only liberate me, it would also have the potential to help others own their stories, too—even if those stories included a fair amount of pain, as did mine. No one's life is free of hurt or struggle. But struggle can equal success. I truly believe that. And I absolutely believe we can take those painful experiences, hold them close, grieve them, and eventually honor them. Then we can embrace every part of ourselves to pursue our dreams and live lives full of love and joy. Sometimes we think the endgame—be it a relationship, a job, a creative endeavor, or whatever it is our heart desires—is where we will find joy. But the joy is also in the journey.

People often mistake vulnerability for weakness. But it is really the complete opposite. It takes incredible strength to be vulnerable, to open yourself wide to potential judgment and scrutiny. To fear that those who have known and loved you will react differently once they hear your *whole* truth. And that was me that morning. Because I was about to share for the first time—in front of 5,000 people, no less—that my personal story—the one that made me who I am today—was also one of bullying, abuse, neglect, betrayal, and codependency. And I hope by telling my truth here—finally, after so many years of pushing it down, pretending it didn't matter—that even just one person might also find the courage to reach out, to embrace their life wholly, and see that *everything* we experience can make us who we are. Because with vulnerability comes strength and the freedom to be who we are destined to be. If we find the clarity and focus in our lives, and the understanding of how to move ahead, we will not get stuck in a dark place, and instead we will realize we have the power within ourselves to find the light. I can't be silent any longer. I must share my story in an effort to help others who may be just as scared as I was for all those years.

You might be thinking why now? The answer is because I finally can.

CHAPTER 1

What Am I Doing Here?

How did I possibly think this was a good idea? I cannot believe I'm doing this. *Deep breath.* Am I *really* back at Port Chester High School, the place where I swore I'd never return? I don't know what's worse—the principal extending an invitation to speak at commencement or my acceptance. Who am I to tell the class of 2007 what they should do next with their lives? Part of me is dying to tell them the bald, unvarnished truth. How about I start with flagrant disregard of responsibility on the part of the staff and administration? Or maybe endangerment of a child would grab their attention. Predatory behavior of teachers? THAT would surely turn some heads. But no, they expect me to come back and talk about my years at school like it was the best time of my life and that none of the bad stuff ever happened.

Inhale serenity, exhale anxiety. Oh, who the hell am I kidding? That Zen stuff sounds great but what I really need is a good stiff drink. Breathe, David. You've been here before. Frayed nerves, churning stomach, the urge to turn tail and run away as fast as possible before they discover I don't belong here.

Glancing up, I see the valedictorian heading to the stage to deliver her speech. I still have some time. The day is warm but that has little to do with why I am breaking out in a sweat. I close my eyes, the voice of the young woman becoming white noise in my head. *Breathe. You've been here before.*

1

• • ● ● ● • •

"David Tutera, please head to the Green Room."

It's 2001, and in a few minutes I'll be on *The View;* LIVE, with five imposing cohosts slinging verbal barbs at each other and likely at me as well. And did I mention intimidating? Barbara Walters was leading the pack back then. I was asked to come on the show to promote my first book, *The Party Planner.* It was early in my career as a party and wedding planner, so I was thankful for the incredible exposure—except I wasn't coming on to talk about planning a party or a wedding. No. I was booked to create five signature cocktails—one for each cohost—on the spot. Live! One teensy-weensy little problem? I wasn't a mixologist! I was petrified.

The morning was a blur: picked up by limo at my apartment in SoHo, being driven to ABC's Studios on Manhattan's Upper West Side with my publicist sitting next to me, talking me off the ledge. We're talking clammy-hands, about-to-puke nerves. As we pulled up to the studio, the crowd of people who were lined up hoping to get in to see the show live started clapping and hooting—until I stepped out of the car. Then I heard the group sigh with disappointment, since they were hoping to catch sight of one of the A-list guests. Well, we were even: They had no idea who I was, and I had no idea how I had landed such an incredible gig!

First-time guests are run through an entire dress rehearsal—lights, camera, and everything. *"Don't look there, look over here!" "Cheat a bit to the left, so the overhead camera can see the cocktail glasses." "Fix that top button on his shirt!"* That took about an hour, then Dana, my producer, walked me past security and to my dressing room. There, on a piece of paper taped to the door, it said: DAVID TUTERA. And that's where I sat for the next three hours wondering how badly I was going to screw this up. By the time my number was up (and believe me, I mean that in every sense of the expression), I honestly didn't think I could go on. But what choice did I have now? I needed a serious talking-to and the only one to do it was me. So, I went into the bathroom and looked straight in the mirror: *"You can do this! You're going to be amazing! Treat this like it's your own damned TV show!"*

And you know what? It worked. And to this day, that has become my routine and my mantra every single time I'm about to walk out onto a stage or in front of a camera.

•• • ● ● • ••

"And now, please welcome back to Port Chester High School, Class of 1984 graduate, our own David Tutera."

Hearing my name snapped me back to attention, and I realized it was my turn to address the graduating class. And as I stepped up to the podium, I repeated the mantra that pulled me through my nerves and anxiety six years earlier.

The principal and his staff—many of whom were teaching when I was a student there in the 1980s—applauded and smiled as I got up to do my thing. I couldn't help thinking that it wasn't my stellar academic career at PCHS that they were applauding, nor any outstanding athletic records I'd left behind. To them, I was simply the local-boy-does-good, returning to the place that "nurtured my talent and prepared me for the future."

Looking out at the sea of young faces, I realized, like that crowd in front of ABC's Studios that morning six years ago, most, if not all of them, had no idea who I was or why I was invited to speak to them. They wouldn't know or care what had happened to me there more than twenty-five years earlier. I couldn't dump my angry baggage on them. But what I *could* do is offer a bit of advice I wish I'd been given: "Don't listen when someone— even a teacher—tells you what you can and can't do if it goes against your instincts and your passions. Everything you've learned and experienced here in this school? You have the opportunity to take what feels right and dismiss what doesn't. Remember that teachers are human. And humans, even well meaning ones, are fallible. They make mistakes like the rest of us, can fail like the rest of us. Be gracious, but be smart and strong."

I wanted to add that when people knowingly and willingly fail you, then you absolutely have a right to be angry. But again, that was MY story and not theirs, or at least I hoped it wasn't. And I hoped they would understand what I was trying to tell them that day.

Coming back to Port Chester is always a difficult experience for me; some of my favorite people are still there, but some of my worst memories are there, too. Port Chester, originally known as Saw Pit, as a nod to its boatbuilding past, is a village of about 25,000 with a small-town vibe and numerous restaurants. The Capitol Theater, just steps away from the train station, makes it a popular destination for NYC day-trippers. It's just a marathon's run from midtown Manhattan, some 26 miles south, but it might as well be light years away culturally, politically, and socially. Sandwiched in lower Westchester County between the affluence of Greenwich, Connecticut, and Rye, Scarsdale, and Purchase, New York, the village has been variously described in *The New York Times* as "hardscrabble," "blue collar," "economically challenged," "ethnically diverse," and a few other euphemisms that invite reading between the lines. The town has always seemed to rebel against change and progress. No matter if you're a candidate with progressive ideas or a super-creative kid who's not into sports and a little different, old ideas die hard in my hometown.

When we're talking family in my old hometown, let's get something straight—you don't just grow up in your own house, you grow up in several houses. You don't just eat dinner at your own home, you eat dinner on a particular night at a particular house—whether it's one set of grandparents or another, your parents' friends, or wherever you get invited. Sunday Dinner was mandatory and don't be late. You know that expression from the Clinton years, "It takes a village?" Port Chester had been practicing that for years. If you lived in one of the real Italian sections of town, you could literally have dinner at a different house each evening, and that was perfectly normal. For me, dinner every Wednesday at Nana and Pop-Pop's was special because it was just the two of them and me—my once-a-week escape from the reality of my dysfunctional home on the other side of town. And if I was truly lucky, there'd be a Sunday dinner as well that week, but that included the rest of my household, so it wasn't nearly as special.

My mother's parents, long since passed, were the light of my life. If things got too heated at home, as they often did, I would stand on the kitchen stool, pick up the phone and call Nana to come pick me up. To this day, I can still remember sleeping in the guest room with my grandmother and listening to the rhythm of her breathing, which calmed me down. As a father, I sometimes share that experience to help my young daughters relax as they begin to fall asleep. It still works for me as well. I have often wished I just could have moved in with Nana and Pop-Pop, but that just wasn't how things were done back then.

Distance, time, experience, and, yes, success, have given me a broader perspective on my hometown. I can return now and realize that my life there and the lessons learned could not have happened in any other place, or with any other people. In much the same way that my first appearance on *The View* was exciting and filled me with fear that I would fail, looking back over my life in Port Chester and beyond, is a mix of mistakes and huge wins. After a few more guest appearances on *The View*, that paper sign on the door with my name on it became an engraved nameplate when I was hired to be a regular. Had I given up, that would not have come to pass. Had I grown up anywhere else, who knows who I would be? As nervous as I was to speak that day at my old high school, in the end, I was pleased with the message I left them with: Do the great things you know you are meant to do; believe in yourself even if no one else does. Eventually, they will have to.

After I delivered that commencement speech, I didn't stick around for the obligatory glad-handing and listening to the teachers who had left me on my own all those years ago telling me, "We knew back then you'd come to be something, and we're so proud of what you're doing now." Instead, I got in my car and drove to Nana and Pop-Pop's home on Smith Street, though now empty of those wonderful, loving spirits. I pulled up to the curb and sighed.

THIS was coming home.

CHAPTER 2
Carpooling With a Corpse

I t's a parent's job to embarrass their children, right? No matter what they do, kids—and especially adolescents—are mortified just by their parents' mere existence. My father, however, took it to an entirely new level. He insisted in dropping me off at middle school . . . in a hearse. And to make matters worse, on more than one occasion, we qualified for the carpool lane, if you know what I mean.

As we passed kids on their way to school, I slunk further and further into the front seat. I begged him to drop me off in front of the Mobil station a block away from school and let me walk the rest of the way. He shrugged off my pleas and instead would pull right up to the front door of Port Chester Middle School. And so my days of being bullied and ridiculed started even before I opened the car door, giving my classmates one more reason to make fun of me.

Our family business was death, and it had a profound impact on me. In fact, I'm sure that being surrounded by so much sadness during those formative years is one reason I determined to make my living—and my life—about celebrating happy times. But it also made me very anxious and instilled in me a deep fear of death and dying that has stayed with me for most of my adult life. I had seen more funerals by the time I was in my teens than most people see in a lifetime. Family business or no, I saw far more than a kid should see long before I really could understand and accept it.

My paternal grandparents originally owned the funeral parlor. For years, my father worked in a very busy funeral home in New York City while also working for his father. Eventually, he took over the business in Port Chester. Like father, like son, like grandson . . . I knew that was the ultimate plan and why my father had started grooming me to move into the family business. Over my dead body, I thought!

When my grandparents were still alive, the funeral home was also *their* home, as in they lived in an apartment right above it. So, visiting them meant also visiting the dead. Ironically the parlor was, and still is, right next to two of Port Chester's most lively places: Cassone's Bakery and the Park Deli. You'd be hard pressed to find anyone from my hometown who doesn't have memories of hitting the bakery after church to get the Italian bread and rolls for Sunday dinner. Parishioners of Corpus Christi Catholic Church, next door to the bakery, had their faith and patience tested as they sat in those pews with the aroma of fresh bread coming in the windows! And Park Deli is still a place you cannot enter without meeting half the town in its narrow, cramped aisles, with everyone catching up as they wait for their soppressata, eggplant and chicken cutlets, cold cuts, and other Italian staples.

Right there, in the middle of it all is the three-story brick building where I learned to hate chrysanthemums and all of the other trappings of death. I never got used to it. All I really wanted was a "normal" family—and even though "normal" is such a subjective and elusive concept, I *knew* my family's life was not normal. It was weird as shit, and I realized it even then. Dinner-table talk was about death and dead bodies. Instead of asking how our day was, or talking about the weather, or even "How 'bout them Mets?" my father would regale us with how a man had died on the toilet (Elvis was not unique in this indignity, it seems) or how he had to drag a body down a staircase because it was too big to carry. Then we heard about how he had to prepare a man who'd had his head blown off (closed casket, thank God) or having to build a special casket for a severely obese corpse.

I mean you can't make this stuff up—and it screwed with my head for years! It took me ten years to do my will because I couldn't decide if I wanted to be buried or cremated. To this day my father *still* makes jokes about his profession. He "puts the *fun* in funeral," as he is fond of saying. (Can you see my eyes rolling?)

I remember all those times going to see my grandparents and catching sight of a corpse laid out in the casket, ready for the wake scheduled later that day. And that was the least upsetting part. For behind the viewing room, separated only by a set of white drapes, was the embalming room where my father would prepare the bodies for viewing. I'll never forget seeing him putting clothes on a body, or putting makeup on a face with unseeing eyes. It still makes me shudder.

It was bad enough to run that gauntlet to visit my grandparents, but then I had to actually work there, helping my father. So I tried to make the best of my inescapable situation by focusing on the one bearable task: making the place look good. Beautiful even. I arranged the carnations and lilies around the casket and the room—and rearranged them until I felt it was a place the mourners could find some solace in their grief. It was that grief that I remember the most—that smothering sadness, the tears and pain of those left behind. The day I had to order a tiny casket for an infant who had died in his sleep devastated me. I was always sensitive and probably even more affected by those feelings than others might be. I mean it never seemed to bother my brother, who still works there alongside my father. Making it worse, I was at an age when I was trying to find fun and happiness and a place with my peers—and here I was, the kid who worked at the funeral home and got dropped off at middle school by a hearse.

Middle school, in my opinion, should be illegal. I don't know if it's hormones, peer pressure, or some toxic mixture of all of the above, but perfectly sweet boys and girls enter sixth grade full of excitement and innocence, and by eighth grade the boys have turned into bullies and the girls are all little witches.

At recess, I liked to play with the girls, and I was an expert at jacks and jump rope. I felt safe with the girls and my best friend was Julie. It was around seventh grade that I began to realize that what I had in common with the girls went beyond playground games. Because when they were giggling and gossiping about the boys they had crushes on . . . I got it! But how in the world could I ever admit that? I didn't even know what do with the feelings that were beginning to take hold. In fact, I really still thought I liked girls in that way, too. I wanted a girlfriend and to kiss her!

Compounding my confusion and anxiety, I was being bullied and rejected by the very boys to whom I was becoming attracted. I wanted them to like me! I tried as best I could to fit in. But I just didn't. I was sensitive, small in stature, and not the least bit athletic. Gym was the absolute worst. I'm sure many can relate to that horrible feeling of always being the last chosen for a team, be it basketball, kickball, or the most dreaded of games: dodgeball. Not only was it humiliating to be picked last, but also adding insult to injury (literally) was getting pummeled by that damned ball. Over and over again.

I am sure that's where my fear and loathing of school really started. But I realize now that it's also when I began to look for, and help, the underdog. I have been there—I know how shitty it feels. So, I seek out the person in a room, the event space, or a party who needs to feel safe and secure. I want them to realize they are fine *just the way they are*. I can't save the world—and it took me a long time to learn how to save myself—but I learned early that if I could make even one person feel better, it lifted me up as well. It's certainly what I wish someone would have done for me back in those middle-school halls.

It wasn't just the humiliation in the gym or at recess. I spent those years as the seeming sole target of my male classmates' verbal and physical abuse. Charlie, Steve, Mike, and the others (all boys) would go out of their way to make my days horrible. It was the beginning of the mental torment and crushing of my heart that would continue throughout my school years.

The first time it happens comes as a shocking blow. Then the second time, and the third, until finally you build your suit of armor, whatever that may be. For me, it was trying to do my very best to appear invisible—walking between classes, head down, peering through my long bangs to see who might be coming my way. I was on the battlefield without any protection. I didn't know how to handle the embarrassment, the name-calling, being shoved into lockers, and being pushed around. I learned fast to never talk back and to just take what was sent my way, and then walk away.

I hoped that if they didn't see me or notice me, I might be safe, able to make it to my next class without hearing "Hey wimp!" "Pussy!" or, finally, "Hey faggot!" At first I had no idea what that word meant, but it didn't take me long to figure it out. Yes. I liked boys. So that made me a faggot? Did they all see that in me before I even realized it? Or was it just the typical name-calling by most middle school boys trying to prove their "manhood?" Funny that I never actually got punched, but I definitely would've preferred a black eye that eventually heals.

Those were the days where bullying was just considered "boys being boys." Even if I had told my teachers or my parents, I know nothing would have changed. Stuff like this was supposed to toughen you up, right? Thank God for the growing awareness of bullying in schools today and for advocacy that didn't exist back then. But I still don't think we are doing enough today. School administration needs to be part of the equation along with teachers and parents. There is a clear connection between being bullied and teenage suicide rates, and we need to do everything possible to make these kids know they can always ask for help. As a dad of two little girls, I want to protect them and make sure they have a safe environment even when I am not with them—especially at school. Every night when I tuck them in, I tell them, "Your two daddies promise to love you, support you, protect you, and guide you." I tell them that no matter what, they can talk to my husband Joey and me—and that they can tell us anything without fear or judgment.

But back in 1979, walking the halls and going out for recess was certainly the worst part of my day. So, it's no surprise that the best part was spent in art, drama, or music classes—subjects that would become such a huge part of my life as I eventually forged my career in wedding and event planning. But back then, they were simply a place where I could express my creativity and soothe my soul. I also started trying out for the choir and school plays. I KNEW I wouldn't run into any of the dodgeball jerks there! But in the end, I did meet someone who would have a profound, lasting and, ultimately, incredibly damaging impact on my life. At first, though, it seemed as if I had found someone who liked me and understood me. It was exactly what I'd been hoping for.

CHAPTER 3
A Wolf in Cheap Clothing

Trying my best to find a place to just fit in *somewhere*, I found singing with the other kids or practicing lines for plays took my mind off the rest of middle school hell, even if it was just until the bell rang, moving us to our next class. For me, getting from one class to the next without being harassed was like an Olympic event. Maybe I learned some useful moves in those dodgeball games after all, for I became a pro at dodging, ducking, and diving to avoid the ever-present bullies, ever ready to lob insults or get in a strategic shove.

I know the whole thing about gay kids migrating to theater and music is a bit of a cliché, but it was definitely true in my case. I was just looking for some sort of safe haven in middle school, and I found it in the choir and in drama class. All of my friends were girls then, and my best friend Julie's mom was the choir director. It seemed natural for me on a lot of levels.

It was during one of these class changes that I saw Mr. English for the first time, probably sometime in early November of my eighth grade year. Talk about not fitting in! Port Chester Middle School was staffed by a cadre of cardigan-clad teacher-moms and middle-aged male instructors with their short-sleeved oxfords, or, if they were a little hipper, polo shirts. But here was this skinny, smiling man wearing a wide-collared qiana shirt (one of those shiny ones popular with the disco crowd) with way too many buttons undone. He had dark curly hair and a thick mustache. Today, the term is "porn 'stache" and, boy, did that turn out to be apropos! Hanging around his neck was a huge silver-and-turquoise necklace, perfectly framed by the V of his open shirt. Mr. English could have been a stunt double for one of the Village People! Plus he was wearing the tightest jeans I've ever seen. Looking back, I have to wonder if the school even *had* a dress code. I'd think that any female teacher wearing similarly suggestive and inappropriate clothing would have been pulled into the principal's office for a dressing down, so to speak, on how to dress up.

I probably stood there in that hall with my eyes wide and my mouth hanging open in astonishment. How had I missed this guy before? Subtlety was clearly not his M.O., in dress, in demeanor, and, as it would turn out, in tenacity. Tragically—although I had *no* clue then—although I would eventually come to discover what he wanted was *me*. But right then, in that hallway, vulnerable and tired of being scared and hurt, when he smiled at me, I thought I had spotted an ally, and maybe even a friend.

Turned out I had to pass Mr. English's classroom several times a day. He would always smile but, strangely enough, never say hello. At least not at first. In retrospect, I honestly think initially he was checking me out, sizing me up—and in some crazy way was playing hard to get. Because after that first time I saw him, I really *did* want to get to know him. Here I am, this confused, and bullied thirteen-year-old who barely even knew what "gay" was; yet I think instinctively I must have known that's what Mr. English was. But he was confident, friendly, AND seemed to fit in! *If he could be like that,* I thought, *then maybe there was hope for me, too.* So, when he started to help out the choir teacher, and then volunteered to help with the school plays, I was excited.

What I didn't know is that he was just as interested in getting to know me as I was in getting to know him. But for all of the wrong reasons. I am pretty sure everyone has a favorite teacher or coach, someone who took them under their wing and helped them blossom or just feel like they had someone to talk to. I like to think that, in the beginning, Mr. English's interest in me was just that innocent and altruistic. But in hindsight, I see now that those days in choir and play practice were the beginning of the end of my innocence. In my naiveté, I thought his attention and friendliness were a godsend. As they say, if I knew then what I know now, I'd have run screaming from the choir room and willingly thrown myself into a game of dodgeball.

As we got further into the school year, rehearsing plays and musicals like *The Boyfriend* and *The Wiz,* I saw Mr. English on a daily basis. Interestingly enough, he became the assistant drama coach. That's when he started to ask me questions about myself, my family, what classes I liked in school (art and music!), and which I didn't (gym!). He would sometimes pull me aside during a break or, when they were rehearsing a scene I wasn't in, run my lines with me one-on-one. *Finally,* I thought, *someone to talk to. Someone who was genuinely interested in me!*

I won't lie. I liked the attention and that he liked me so much. Julie hung out with us too during those rehearsals. It was like the three of us had our own private club, and I loved it! I was accepted and finally started to feel like school wasn't just unending torture. There was something to look forward to—Mr. English and Julie.

After a while, it wasn't just during choir and play practice that we got together. Sometimes we'd go off campus, the three of us, to get a burger or go for ice cream. Julie's mom knew Mr. English and so had no problem with him taking us around. I still had to work with my father at the funeral home, but having these best friends, even one nearly twenty years my senior, seemed to make even those horrible chores more bearable. Today, there's no way in the world a teacher would spend time alone with students after school, at least not without another adult chaperone. But back then we thought nothing of it. Nor did my parents.

Don't get me wrong. It wasn't suddenly all sunshine and rainbows. My father still dropped me off at school in the hearse, and I still had to run the gauntlet of the taunts and shoves as I made my way to my locker. I still started out my days holding my breath, feeling every ounce of the anxiety and stress that no kid should ever have to feel. I will say, however, that one segment of the student body that I never feared, that never bullied me, and with whom I felt totally at ease, were the Black kids. This was in the late '70s and early '80s, so the worst of the racial tensions were behind us as Port Chester had evolved from a town that was predominantly Italian, a little Polish, a lot Catholic, and a dash of Jewish, to a more diverse population that included a growing number of Black and Hispanic families.

I was interviewed in 2006 by a Black reporter about my TV show *My Fair Wedding,* and she asked me why I thought I connected so well with the Black community. I had never really thought about it. She said that when my audience watched and listened to me, they saw that I was looking at a Black bride as a person and not as a Black person. I still appreciate her insight, and it has helped me look back and find a little more peace with that time in my life.

So, while I still spent a good part of every day pretending not to hear the things my classmates would say to me, I did start to hear something new in their nasty comments. I had gotten pretty good at ignoring the "fag" and "sissy" remarks—but then I heard one of the boys say something about my "new boyfriend." I didn't know what the hell that was about, but when they pegged me for gay, years before I even knew it, apparently they noticed something about Mr. English.

Every kid looks forward to that last day of school, but for me it was like being released from prison. I could not wait for summer! Not only would I be free from the daily assaults, but also this summer Mr. English, Julie, and I had plans! We were going to have a blast. During the school year, Mr. English had started taking Julie and me to movies, treating us to lunch and dinner. But over the summer, he promised to take us to the beach as much as we wanted, to plays in Manhattan, and so much more. Looking back with the hindsight of an adult—and as a parent—I see now how odd and inappropriate that was. Weren't most boys my age hanging out with their peers? Riding bikes and playing baseball? (Well, okay, playing baseball was never going to be a part of my daily routine, but you get what I'm saying.)

But at the time, I was just living in the moment and looking forward to the summer ahead.

What's funny is I still thought Julie would be my real girlfriend one day, and so I also naively thought Mr. English was just helping pave the way by taking us together everywhere that summer. Like a lot of gay adolescents, I still wasn't sure of my sexuality. *Maybe once I kissed Julie and she would be my girlfriend,* I reasoned, *I'd stop being attracted to boys.* But at the time I was just enjoying the attention and the best summer ever.

A favorite destination for the three of us was the beach. Mr. English loved to work on his tan and would lay there on his towel in the tiniest of Speedos. The closest beach to us was Rye Beach, right in front of Playland Amusement Park, with its famous Dragon Coaster (remember *Fatal Attraction*?) and its beautiful art deco buildings. Mr. English would pick us up by mid-morning, already in our bathing suits, with towels and lunches in hand. Julie always sat in the backseat and I rode shotgun.

The first time it happened I thought it was an accident. That his hand must have just slipped off the gearshift and grazed my bare thigh. But when it happened again, and he left his hand there for a few seconds, I froze. I looked over at him, and he smiled at me. I realized then it was no accident. What I didn't realize was that was just the beginning.

CHAPTER 4
Nowhere to Run

To this day I will never understand how my father let Mr. English pull one over on him. For a man who prided himself on being in charge, a decision-maker, and a buck-stops-here kind of guy, he never realized this bold, flamboyant teacher who breezed into our home and lives did not belong there. And I mean Mr. English literally breezed into our home. He just started coming by one day toward the end of eighth grade, and by the time summer vacation started, he was a regular fixture in our house. He'd stay for dinner, swim in our pool, and generally, as I see now, insinuate himself into my life.

Clearly my parents had to know Mr. English was gay. I mean between the Freddy Mercury mustache, conspicuous wardrobe, and overt mannerisms, he might as well have had a neon sign on his forehead. In all fairness, my parents were completely unaware of my own confusion surrounding my sexuality (even I was still confused!), so it never occurred to them for a moment that Mr. English was basically "grooming me," in today's vernacular. Even still, the fact that they didn't question this man's ever-growing presence in our home and in my life confounds me. Would my parents have been so welcoming had I been a young girl instead of a young man? Hard to say. Teachers hold a special place in our society. We look up to them. We listen to them. We believe they have the best interests of our children at heart. In a word, we trust them. This was especially true back in the 1970s and early 1980s, before we started hearing about teachers having affairs with students (and even babies—remember Mary Kay Letourneau who became pregnant by her underage student?) and the explosive revelations of child sexual abuse in the Catholic Church and schools.

From that first day of kindergarten throughout the next twelve years, when we send our children to school, we are taking this enormous leap of faith that, aside from their official role of academic instruction, teachers will care for our children and protect them. We trust them to get our children to safety during a fire drill and, sadly these days, during the far-too-frequent lockdowns in the event of an active shooter. And certainly the overwhelming majority of teachers assume that responsibility.

Teachers have acquired this aura of wisdom, experience, and a "teacher-knows-best" quality. And when one teacher starts to pay special attention to our child, as a parent we feel honored that our child has been singled out. Our kid must really be super fill-in-the-blank: smart, talented, above average, showing promise, too bored by the regular curriculum, etc. Obviously, that *must* be why this teacher is taking his or her personal time to give *my* child extra attention.

And Mr. English used that mentality to con my parents into trusting him to spend more time with me. In school, I was getting much more involved in theatre, so it made perfect sense for Mr. English to foster my interest (and "talent"! Stroke that parental ego!) by treating Julie and me to see Broadway shows. The first trip was to see *A Chorus Line*, which had only been running for a few years and was still one of NYC's hottest tickets. And it really *did* foster my interest in theatre . . . but it also was the real start of when Mr. English essentially began to insert himself into every aspect of my life—with my parents' blessing.

That summer, and through the following school year, was when the various threads of my life converged and entwined, and—as I can see now with a clarity and self-awareness that is completely absent in any thirteen-year-old—began to shape who I would eventually become as a person. While my father seemed oblivious to Mr. English's inappropriate insinuation into my life, he nevertheless continued to control *my* life path because he was absolutely determined that I would one day take over the family business. I can never forget all the times my father would interrupt whatever was going on to announce he "just got a death call"—as if God himself had rung up my father to entrust him with all the messy stuff until it was His turn to step in. What I heard was there was yet another funeral in my near future—and the dread that never seemed to totally abate intensified.

By this time, I was serving as a regular pallbearer. Remember that when funerals are held in a funeral home, and not a church, the casket is already in place by the time the mourners arrive. The other pall bearers and I would haul the casket from the hearse, down the aisle, and place it onto the catafalque, then duck out the side entrance to the deli next door and wait over a cup of coffee or a bagel until it was time to reverse our path. We also accompanied the funeral procession to the cemetery and carried the casket to the grave. It always astounded me how stoic and detached and unaffected the other pallbearers were by this job. I was by far the youngest—and smallest—pallbearer on the payroll (oh, wait—I didn't ever get paid) and, much to the chagrin of my father, the most sensitive. I simply could not see this as "just a job" and was emotionally affected by every single funeral. I would ask my father the name of the person, how old they were, what family was left behind . . . and by the time I was helping to carry the casket down the aisle, I was crying, which annoyed the hell out of my father. "Just carry the damned casket," he'd scream.

My father always identified the deceased by how they died: "a suicide," "severed head in a motorcycle crash," "crib death," "heart attack on the toilet." And, of course, how a person died dictated the type of work that would be needed to prepare them for viewing, except for the cases when an open casket was definitely not an option. The entire time I had to work in that place, I never once crossed behind that white curtain into the embalming room, despite constant badgering and sometimes-angry orders from my father to do so. I think he believed if I could become desensitized, I would eventually give up and join the local chapter of the Future Funeral

Directors of America. It was one of the biggest battles I ever won with my father, though it was a few years before I completely severed those family-business ties.

I can see that in order to deal with death on a daily basis, as my father and his father did, depersonalizing it like this was a way to be able to handle such a difficult job. But that was exactly why I knew, even then, that I absolutely could not follow in my father's footsteps. Don't get me wrong. I really do appreciate the dedication and responsibility it takes to grow and maintain a family business, and why it was so important to my father to want to bring me into it as his eldest son. But it was never, ever something I could do. But what I *could* do, and pretty much the only thing about the funeral home I could stomach and, in fact, came to enjoy, was arranging the flowers. I threw myself into making sure that a place of such sadness could at least be beautiful—as a tribute to honor the deceased and as a way to at least partially soothe those left behind. I'd take the arrangements that poured in before a funeral and purposefully and mindfully place, and re-place them, around the parlor and the casket until I was satisfied that the room looked the very best it could be. And, coincidentally, quite a number of those flowers came from my maternal grandfather Pop-Pop's florist shop, Moraio Brothers, on Purchase Street in Rye, New York.

At the same time I was working for my paternal grandfather in the funeral business I was also working with Pop-Pop my maternal grandfather, who owned the floral shop. I was sixteen, and I am certain that that experience directly influenced my future passions and career. At first, of course, I did the grunt work— sweeping out the trimmings on the floor, cleaning out the flower coolers, tidying up the benches of stray ribbons, cards, and such. Eventually I started manning the phones, along with two dear women, Ann and Barbara, who adored my grandfather and worked for him for years. These days it's hard to imagine a time when you didn't just type in Flowers.com or 1-800-Flowers.com and place your own order. But back then, FTD was the only game in town, and I spent countless hours taking orders and finding florists shops around the country to create and deliver the non-local orders. For one thing, it was a terrific way to hone my communication skills. For another, I received an amazing education about flowers! The myriad varieties, which ones went best together, how a florist improvises if they don't have the exact materials to match the photo or description of an arrangement—in short, so many of the skills I would use when I began my event-planning business.

What is ironic, and frustrated the hell out of me as much as I loved and appreciated my dear Pop-Pop, rest his soul, is that no matter how many times I asked and begged, he never once let me make an arrangement. People are stunned when I tell them this (*I'm* still stunned by it). But Pop-Pop took his business very seriously, and only a trained florist, which I was not and neither was he, created the bouquets or sprays. People were paying for that service, and that's what they got—not an eager thirteen- or four- teen- or even fifteen-year-old who wanted to give it a try.

He was a businessman through and through, and I have carried his wisdom and experience with me from those days forward. Pop-Pop made me pay my dues. When I was nineteen, and had the opportunity to buy my own singing telegram business, he loaned me the money to do so. And realiz- ing I was serious about things, he sat me down and explained purchasing, balancing inventory, cash flow, and recipes for keeping those flowers fresh. Because if those perishables went bad, he explained, you were out of busi- ness. "Profits from perishables," he called it.

Funny, but I never realized until now how that statement applied to my father's business as well.

CHAPTER 5

Nowhere to Hide

Mr. English made it his mission to be my first: my first Broadway show; my first time behind the wheel of a car; my first lead role in a high school play; my first time at a gay beach; my first time at a gay club (the latter two completely unbeknownst to me until I was there, shocked and looking to escape). But his ultimate goal was to really be my FIRST.

All that summer and through ninth grade, there were more trips to the local beach, more Broadway shows, more lunches and dinners (all with Julie accompanying us, which leant an artificial sense of decorum and safety, I see now). I began to feel uncomfortable with Mr. English's attention toward me. Causing further uneasiness were the increasingly frequent "accidental" brushes against my leg and even my crotch while I was riding shotgun in his little red MG. One time I actually started to get an erection when he brushed his hand against me and I tried to hide it, embarrassed and confused. I was still just as naive as ever and had no one to talk to about it. God forbid my parents would ever talk to me about my body or puberty or sex. So when my body had a totally correct reaction to a totally incorrect stimulus, I had no idea what to do.

At school, the whispers grew louder that there was something going on between Mr. English and me. The usual bullies continued to refer to him as "my boyfriend." I tried to ignore these comments as best I could, but looking back, why wouldn't they think that? But more important, if the students thought something was off, why didn't the teachers or administration notice what was going on? I imagine they thought that if my parents didn't seem to have an issue with Mr. English, who were they to intervene? Making matters worse, he offered to help my mother plan my father's surprise fortieth birthday party, further ingratiating himself into our family.

Mr. English was my ninth grade English teacher and still helped out with the choir and drama, the two extracurricular activities that I actually took part in and enjoyed. This, of course, meant he was a constant presence in school, and he made a point of being a constant presence outside of it as well. The attention he gave me—and my feelings about it—were completely double edged. Of course I enjoyed being taken to shows and being driven to school in a sports car instead of a hearse. And even his frequent visits to our home served as a buffer—my father was less inclined to bully and berate us and was generally on better behavior when we had company.

But by the time I was about to enter high school, I was really ready for a break. I needed space and distance from Mr. English, and I was looking forward leaving him behind. Starting high school is such a seminal event for any kid. It's like you can see the light at the end of the tunnel that represents your future—it's still a ways off but gives you something to shoot for.

But any sense of promise and excitement was short-lived. Because guess who was coming to high school? I found out on Day 1 that Mr. English had transferred to the high school as an English teacher and as the assistant to the drama director. *Of course,* I was in his freshman English class. And because there was only one drama department, he knew he'd find me there as well. I couldn't believe it—was he actually *following* me to high school? Why hadn't he told me about it? It's not like he hadn't had plenty of opportunities over the summer. If he thought I was going to be pleasantly surprised, he couldn't have been more wrong.

Something shifted in me at that moment, and I adopted an attitude that was at once defiant and determined, yet defeated and resigned. I clearly couldn't even avoid him in school now, so I accepted his self-appointed role in my life, thinking I could handle it. I'd become adept at ignoring the snide rumors and insults. (I knew none of what they said was true.) And I did get some tangible benefits from his attention, so how much worse could it get?

In his own twisted way, I think Mr. English thought he was doing me a favor. Take the obvious (but still oblivious) gay kid under his wing and guide him. It was as if he was teaching "How to Be Gay 101" to a class of one. I was neither a very good nor a very willing student, for which I am grateful. In his eyes, especially during that time, all gay men were promiscuous and devil-may-care, and the gay lifestyle was solely one of irresponsibility and recklessness. Thankfully, I eventually discovered that wasn't true at all, but it would take me many years of experience and therapy to learn that lesson. But then, in the early '80s—right on the cusp of the AIDS epidemic—Mr. English introduced me to some of the worst aspects that gay life had to offer.

Sherwood Island State Park, adjacent to one of Connecticut's toniest towns, Westport, is a short drive down I-95 from Port Chester. Right on Long Island Sound, it features a picnic pavilion, places to fish and hike, and two beaches: West Beach and East Beach. It was a favorite destination for Mr. English and, of course, he made a point of bringing me there. It was my first gay beach, although I had no idea what it was at the time. I thought we were just heading to the shore as usual, except this day Julie wasn't with us. Upon entering, he told me to turn left—toward East Beach—and I soon found out why. Clad in his ridiculously tiny Speedo to show off how well-endowed he was, he fit right in with every other man there. There were no women (you had to turn *right* to get to the family beach). After spreading out our towels on the sand, he told me he'd be back in a bit, that he was headed to the bathrooms to get a blow job. Just like that. For all his prior subtlety and innuendoes over the last year, he was suddenly unabashedly graphic and bold. Mr. English went on to tell me that for more "involved" encounters, men went to the far parking lot to hook up. Did he think I was taking notes?

So there I sat on my towel, holding my knees against my skinny chest, looking out at the ocean but also casting sidelong glances at the other men on the beach, wondering if THIS was what was in store for me if I really was gay? Because at nearly fourteen, I still wasn't really sure. I knew I was attracted to boys (but NEVER to Mr. English), but I was also attracted to girls. To say that day on the beach was both shocking and intriguing would be an understatement.

Always one to try to outdo himself, the next rung up from taking me to my first gay beach was taking me to my first gay club. Again, I was clueless until I was standing in the middle of The Swamp, an iconic gay hangout in East Hampton, New York. And because Julie accompanied us on that trip, it was the last thing I expected. But Mr. English had no shame or scruples. I mean, who would take two fourteen-year-olds to a Hamptons' gay bar, especially when one of them was a girl? But for Julie and me, we were just excited to be going to a club, leaving the moral and legal ramifications to our "chaperone." And this is the thing that still blows me away—I was a kid. Julie was a kid. Where were the grownups? Where was the culpability when a teacher takes two underage students to a gay bar AND shares a motel room with them? The honest answer is there were many rumors, plenty based on fact as I know now, of inappropriate teacher-student relationships going on at Port Chester High School while I was a student. Turning a blind eye was the status quo because if someone called out one teacher, how many more would he in turn point the finger at?

High school for me was something to just get through, to be endured. My grades were average, I played no sports (a definite eyebrow raiser among the school's many jocks), and the debate club was the only club I joined. It's an unwritten rule that everyone in Port Chester takes part in one of the school bands. It was true then, and, from what I hear, is still true now. Important events were and still are planned around band events. So, I played clarinet and saxophone in the marching band, then finally landed the position of drum major during my junior and senior years. The drum major, of course, is basically in charge of getting the band into position, running rehearsals, being a little bit bossy, and ensuring everyone and everything is where they need to be at show time. Hmmm. Guess I was getting pretty good practice for my eventual career as an event and wedding planner, even though I didn't know it then! Of course, it was no surprise to me when Mr. English started volunteering to chaperone our band trips. I wasn't pleased about it because those were some really fun trips to places like Quebec and Toronto, and would have been that much better if my thirty-five-year-old shadow hadn't been along for the ride.

After school, I still worked with my grandfather at the florist shop, and less and less with my father, who seemed to be accepting the fact I was not picking up *that* baton. But for the most part, performing in the plays and musicals was how I spent most of my time outside the classroom. Anyone who has been involved in drama in high school knows you work your way up the ranks to those coveted lead roles. First year you're in the chorus, then you might get a small speaking or singing part the following year, and then eventually you're in line for one of the leads by senior year, junior year if you're lucky. I like to think that my talent and enthusiasm alone garnered me the choice roles I started landing, but I know Mr. English was driving the bus, especially when he moved from assistant to director of the drama department my second year when the original director left.

Rumors of favoritism abounded, and I can't say they weren't at least partially true. Mr. English would flat out ask me what plays and what roles I'd like, and, voila, that was what we performed. I played Romeo in *Romeo and Juliet*, Barnum in *Barnum*, the Lead Player in *Pippen*—yet I believed then and now that other students would have done as well or better than me in the roles. In fact, two of my classmates and fellow thespians went on to become very successful actors in movies, television, and on stage, so their talent was clearly evident, even in high school. Looking back, I get angry at how Mr. English's machinations created an atmosphere of animosity and competition between me and these two classmates, who were gay (though not openly at that time) and wonderful actors. We could have been friends and allies, but they disliked me—and I can't say I blame them.

Port Chester, being as close as it is to New York City, made it easy for me to start going to auditions, beginning around the time I was sixteen. While drama started out as just a haven from the jerks in middle school, by the time I was midway through high school, I was seriously considering acting as a career. Not only did I enjoy the audition process and the possibility of landing some parts, either in commercials or actual shows, it also served as a way for me to get the hell off campus the moment the dismissal bell rang.

Despite my strained relationship with my father, he was always willing to drive me to auditions if his schedule allowed (i.e., no "death calls!"). We never actually talked about it, but it felt to me like it was his way of showing his acceptance, if not total support, for my choice to not take over the funeral home. I appreciated those rides, which gave me a chance to see a softer side of my father than I usually did.

Often, I just hopped on the train for the hour-long ride to the city, and I relished the rare opportunity to just be alone. No classmates, no parents or siblings, no Mr. English. It was wonderful. But Mr. English found out about my dashing after class to make the train, and the next thing I knew, he was dashing out the door right after me, insisting on giving me rides.

I did get a few parts in commercials and movies. Maybe it was the confidence I was gaining from those auditions, coupled with the school plays and being the drum major—and maybe it was just simply maturing—but I felt a real shift in my relationship with Mr. English. I had moved from being wary of him to being annoyed and angry. I guess in some way I also felt completely justified taking advantage of him. If he wanted to haul me down to the city for auditions, fine with me! Saved me the train fare. I knew what he ultimately wanted from me—a sexual and emotional relationship—was never going to happen. I began to see him as less threatening and more as pathetic.

Even though it was becoming more clear to me that I was gay, my first sexual encounter was with a girl. As with many teenaged boys, it was a fumbling episode upstairs during a party when I was sixteen. The sex was forgettable but the case of crabs was not. And in a cruel parallel years later, I got crabs the first time I had sex with a man as well. This, among other more serious things, probably started what would be a lifelong anxiety and fear of sex.

Regardless, I did date girls during high school and even went to the prom every year, each time with a different girl who asked me to be her date. I had a great time with each of them, but as with seemingly every other activity, Mr. English was looming. He was on the prom planning committees, and he chaperoned each one as well. One prom in particular has stayed in my memory, held at one of the beautiful waterside party venues in New Rochelle, New York. (The same ones where the big bands and crooners from the 1950s used to perform to audiences of bejeweled, gowned women and their tuxedoed dates.) All night long, I knew I was being watched. Mr. English stood at the side of the ballroom like a wallflower when my date and I were dancing; and if we moved to another place on the dance floor, he'd reposition himself for a better view. Popped over to the punch bowl? Guess who was also filling his glass? It was creepy and disconcerting. I don't think the term "stalker" was in common use then, but Mr. English's picture could have accompanied any dictionary definition.

At one point, in desperation, I actually contacted Mr. English's ex-wife, which, when I think about it now, was a pretty bold move for a teenager. She wasn't surprised by his attentions toward me and very nonchalantly informed me I wasn't the first student he'd focused on. God only knows what kind of a relationship they had during and after their marriage, but for her to not only be aware of but unbothered by his actions still floors me. Plus, I was disheartened. Here I had finally gotten the nerve to talk to an adult about the situation and she shrugged it off. And it wouldn't be the last time I encountered a similar reaction.

Something I had kept secret from everyone was that from the time I was in middle school, Mr. English had written me letters. At first, they were real rah-rah, hang-in-there notes that, by comparison to what they would become in late high school, were almost quaint. There's nothing wrong with a teacher giving a student an encouraging word, but the fact he would slip these letters to me in a book or pass them off to me in the hallway leant an icky "just our little secret" quality to them. I would take them home, go up to my room, and, after reading them, tear them into a million pieces and throw them away. Despite the initial innocent messages, I knew there was just something totally wrong about them. I had no idea just how wrong they would become.

As I said before, I knew what Mr. English wanted from me and, as I got older and more mature, his desire and efforts grew. He never overtly physically accosted me (aside from those "accidental" touches), but in some ways I think that would have been easier to handle than the drip, drip, drip of his constant, smothering presence; the favoritism and gifts (did I mention he always gave me an expensive and elaborate gift on the closing nights of every play I was in?); and the feeling that I could never, ever do anything that he wouldn't find a way to take part in. And the letters—those horrible, anxiety-producing letters. The content of the letters graduated from relatively innocuous to uncomfortable flattery. Then probably about the same time as he started "teaching" me about what it was, in his mind, to be gay, he turned to plying me with personal self-flattery, in graphic detail: the hookups at clubs, the orgies, the drugs, the penis size of his latest sex partner, HIS penis size. Only someone beyond narcissistic and sick would think for a second that this would impress anyone. It disgusted me. I continued to destroy the letters. I wish I'd had the strength to just throw them away unopened. But like watching a train wreck, there was this morbid fascination that compelled me to read them.

By the time my senior year rolled around, the letters became worse than I could imagine. Not only did they increase in frequency, but the words were desperate, pleading, and threatening. He confided in me that he'd contracted HIV and that he needed me to be with him and take care of him. He threatened to commit suicide if I didn't finally give in to him. *That* was the last straw—the thing that finally pushed me past the shame and embarrassment to talk to the high school guidance counselor about him.

And the counselor's reaction? Nothing. Not a goddamned thing. So next I went to the principal with the same information. Again, another big shrug by an adult who was supposed to be in charge, protecting the students. Finally, I decided to take it all the way up the chain of command to the superintendent, who also happened to be a close friend of my grandparents. She dismissed me out of hand. Hell, the man was threatening suicide, and, serious or not, they didn't even care about that. Fuck it. I did my due diligence.

I didn't get the help I wanted and deserved that day—but I found strength that I didn't know I had. Sitting there baring my soul, I realized the only one who was going to help me was me. Graduation was getting near, and I could almost taste the freedom—freedom from this school and from Mr. English, finally. No way in hell was he following me into the next stage of my life, even though I wasn't quite sure what that would be.

But I still had classes to finish, including AP Literature, which I had with Mrs. Harris, a middle-aged teacher. She had a reputation as being one of the bitchiest teachers in the school, yet she was extremely friendly to me, especially as the school year was winding down. I was too preoccupied with all of my senior-year activities to give it much thought. And because English was one of my better subjects, I was frustrated when she would continually keep me behind in class to work on my assignments. Finally, she told me that I should come by her house one night so she could give me the extra help I needed to pass the course.

When I arrived, there were candles lit all over the place and she offered me a glass of wine, despite my being underage. She insisted on giving me a tour of the house, culminating in her bedroom. At that point, she went full-on Mrs. Robinson, not even trying to pretend why she invited me over. Keep in mind she was not only my teacher, but a married one at that. And I was still only seventeen. But the real pisser? She informed me that she and Mr. English had a long-standing bet as to which of them would have sex with me first. I had heard rumors that she'd had sex with other male students, but didn't believe it until that night, when I joined the club. (At least I didn't get crabs!) Twisted as it was, I was only too happy to help her win the bet. It was the best fuck-you, parting "gift" to Mr. English I could imagine. Not only was he not my first, he would never have any part of me ever again.

CHAPTER 6
It's All About Family

T he backdrop to everyone's story is, of course, their family. Good, bad, tragic, fairy tale—no matter how we label our lives, the facts and stories of our family is where it all starts. What I've recounted so far in this book are some of the hardest, most painful memories of my formative years, but while my family often caused me great pain, there was also love and nurturing, particularly from my maternal grandparents.

I have always wondered what a traditional family is supposed to feel like. Looking back, I think anyone on the outside looking in would have thought we were "traditional": father who worked, mother who stayed home to raise the kids when we were young, Sunday dinners, backyard swimming pool. But in reality, we were a dysfunctional family before that was even a label.

It's difficult to go back to the past when you know it's likely to be a bad trip. Memories are that double-edged sword: we romanticize the pleasant ones and try to forget the bad ones. But so often it is the unpleasant ones that have the most to teach us. We carry memories of our family for our entire lives. Even those that are buried deep—consciously or subconsciously— are a constant reminder of who we turned out to be.

I have spent countless hours since I was a young adult trying to best understand my family dynamic and how it impacted me. It was my daughter Cielo's natural curiosity about my side of the family that opened my mind and provided much-needed clarity about my childhood. When I tuck Cielo into bed, she loves for me to tell her stories of when I was a child.

"Daddy, tell me a story of when you were a kid, but don't tell me the same story again. I want to hear a new one tonight."

This started when she was about three years old. At first, it seemed like a wonderful way to share great stories and bring her into my childhood. Plus, it would help her better know her grandparents and my siblings, who all still lived across the country, still in Port Chester. As the bedtime stories continued over a few months, I realized my library of stories was finite. I had few new stories to share (much to the chagrin of Cielo!), so gradually the stories I shared with her morphed into those I made up—stories of what I *wished* my childhood had been. I can see it now as "accidental therapy." While that was never my intention, it forced me to look hard at what I recalled.

The happy memories of my childhood center primarily on my mother and her parents, Nana and Pop-Pop. These two remarkable people helped me become who I am today, and not just because Pop-Pop taught me all about the floral industry and loaned me the money for my first company. Or that Nana would swing by and whisk me away to go shopping with her. (Retail therapy was in my blood even then!) But it was their love and their brilliant ways of teaching simple life lessons that have stayed with me to this day, and this is what I am passing along to both my girls. They were my sanity and my safety, and I thank God I had them in my life.

Mary Rita Corsaro—Nana—was a bold, brassy, and kind woman. She cared, she loved, she was present, and she spoke her mind. Nana said what she meant and told you what you needed to know, whether you wanted to hear it or not. Her love for life was contagious, and man how she loved her friends—Dottie, Tuts, Daisy, and the rest—and man did they love to have fun. For example, Nana loved to sneak out late at night. She would put a change of clothes in the trunk of the car, and, after sharing dinner with Pop-Pop and waiting until he'd fallen asleep after a long day of work, off she would go to pick up the rest of her "delinquent" gang! They'd go to a restaurant or local bar to just drink and laugh and be silly. (Incidentally, I had my first sip of an alcoholic drink with my grandparents: a gin and tonic with a slice of lime—still a favorite of mine.)

I loved to hear her stories and see the sparkle in her eye when she shared those moments. Nana also loved casinos, loved cruises, loved the Catskills. But she did NOT love Florida, not one little bit. But she loved my grandfather and so went with him because Pop-Pop loved to golf.

Pop-Pop—Joseph Corsaro—was a man of few words. But he dove right in to teach me how to start and run my business. He was filled with nuggets of golden information and played such an important role in those early days while I was starting my career. I am forever grateful to them both for stepping in, caring, and helping me along the way.

While my entire family would frequently go to my grandparents' home for Sunday dinner and feast on Nana's epic meatballs, pasta, and Italian wedding soup, Wednesday nights I had my grandparents to myself. First, we'd play canasta (does anyone even know what that is today?) and then eat overdone chicken cutlets. I couldn't have been happier. It was their love and connection that nourished me and stays with me to this day. I mentioned before that I would often call Nana to come get me when I needed to get away from home. *Their* home was my safe space. Even when we would take trips as a family—my parents, sister and brother, Nana and Pop-Pop, and me—I would always stay in my grandparents' hotel room.

• • ● ● ● • •

I was influenced and affected by my father, of course, as he inevitably was by his father. The big difference is I have always been *escaping* my father's influences and behaviors so as not to be shaped by them. I am my not my father's boy, and he never accepted that. I was not the son he thought he'd have, I guess. Not an athlete by any stretch himself, he nevertheless bought me the requisite "boy" props: footballs, baseballs, and other trappings he believed a son should have to prove that he's a young man. I found out once that my father gave my cousin a football that was never used by me, so he must have seen the writing on the wall, even if he didn't like the message.

My father and I have nothing in common now and really never did, but not for lack of trying on my part. He was the dominant figure in our family of three, then four, then five. Even today, with a family that now includes grandchildren and a wife who is not well, my father still clings to whatever hold on us he has left. As much as I'm not the product of my father, I do take one positive attribute from him—he had, and continues to have, a tenacious work ethic. He took me to my first jobs, my first auditions in the city, and seemed to *want* to do these things for me. (Coincidentally, both our respective careers began within the Jewish community—his with a funeral home on Manhattan's Upper East Side; mine with the woman who hired me for my first bar mitzvah job, even though I didn't know what that was! But that's a story for later.) Believe me, I wish there were more positive things that I could list about my father. I remember desperately wishing and hoping to find good takeaways from our relationship in those days, but the only thing I kept taking away was frustration and disappointment and a wish for more connection, more acceptance, and more kindness.

What I did come to understand is his ideals and beliefs were not something to emulate and they came from his own family. My father's father was a racist of the first degree, with aggression and nastiness toward others of any race thrown in for good measure. The slang words that flew throughout my life still make me cringe. If you were not white or Catholic, you were something else. My grandfather had a name for African Americans, for Hispanics, for Jews—and God forbid if you were gay. Archie Bunker had nothing on him.

He despised Mom's side of the family—even Nana and Pop-Pop—and I'll never know why. He called my Aunt Maria a "black swan." (What the hell does that even mean? Did he confuse it with "black sheep?") And the way he treated my mother was inexcusable. My father's parents were rude, unkind, and flat-out nasty to my mother—and yet she never spoke back. Not ever. (Nor did my father ever defend my mother, but that's all part of the dysfunction.)

One evening when my grandparents were at the dining room table in our little home, my grandfather called my mom stupid, in his arrogant and horrible tone. I just lost my seventeen-year-old shit, walked into the dining room and yelled at him, and told him to never ever speak to my mother like that again. "You are a horrible man, and *you* are the one that should be called stupid. I will never, ever speak to you again for how you have treated my mom all the years I can remember." And it was the last time I spoke to him.

At least seeing how my father was shaped helped me make sense of it all so that I could stop taking it personally. Being raised in such a blatantly racist and dominating environment, it's clear that what my father absorbed in his formative years was all he knew. Not only was therapy and self-awareness not even on the radar back then (or when I was a young man, for that matter), but any acknowledgment of "something wrong" with yourself or your family was seen as a sign of weakness, especially in an old Italian family like ours. What my father learned about being a father he naturally deposited onto his own children years later. But you can bet that with me now being a father of two that cycle has stopped. My goal has always been to break the cycle—to change the future to allow my family to flourish. My main focus is for my husband and my daughters to live a life filled with love and to know that together we are all here to support, to protect, to guide, to listen, and to love one another for all that we are.

I can't ever prove this about my father, and he would never admit it, but I believe that he was envious of my success in my chosen field, and it began early. I can understand jealousy among peers, among friends, even among siblings, but . . . from *my own father*? Mom was so proud of all I'd accomplished. So why wasn't *he* proud of my work ethic, my dedication to details, and getting things done—all traits that he exemplified, and that he passed to me? Wasn't he happy that I *wasn't* dependent upon him? Here I was, the eldest child that *didn't* need him the way the other family members did, and this must have messed with his need to control me to no end. Unfortunately, this led to arguments, tirades, purposeful miscommunication, and petulant, passive-aggressive behavior. Oh, and let's add in the fact that his son is a homosexual—a reality he has never come to terms with. I'll never forget his demeanor at my wedding—one of the happiest days of my life—and there's my father, head in his hands, looking more like he was attending a funeral. Ironic.

I found out later that it wasn't only my dad who resented me; my sister laid it on me as well. Apparently, according to her, I "sucked the success out of her and my brother." Who knew there was only a finite amount of success to go around among siblings? This hurt me almost as much as realizing my father resented me. Apparently, the only one in my immediate family who didn't resent me was my mom. And for that reason alone, over the years, we grew closer and more supportive of each other.

The codependency my father instilled in each of us manifested itself differently. My younger brother is the "good" son, the one who follows dad's direction. Entirely dependent on our father for everything, he lives under his roof, works for him and always has (giving my father one thing I never could). I worry and have no clue what he will do when my parents are gone.

My brother definitely has friends, a social life, loves sports, and going to the casinos, so I am not saying he is unhappy. In fact, I think he might be the most contented one in our family, but I can't help but wonder what might have been if my father hadn't molded him the way *he* wanted him to be. My brother never had the opportunity to forge his own path, and, honestly, I don't think that has ever bothered him because it's all he's ever known. When thinking about what my sister said about my "sucking the success" out of the family, it's so hard for me to believe my brother feels like that toward me. Like Pop-Pop, he's a man of few words and almost none of them are mean. It might have just been my sister's way of trying to make me feel bad (and it did).

My mother survived a bout of cancer years ago, and that was obviously a difficult time for her. I had her move in with me in New York City for a month and then up to my place in rural Connecticut after that. I just wanted her to recover in peace, and that was impossible in Port Chester, where my sister was creating chaos and drama and nothing but stress for my parents. She found ways to bring all the attention to her issues (which she created each and every time). My sister has always been that sixteen-year-old that never grew up with a sense that everyone must take care of *her*. After her divorce, she placed responsibility of her two young kids on my parents' laps, literally. There's nothing wrong with family stepping in to help following something as difficult as becoming a single parent. In fact, that's what healthy families do: support you when you need it most until you're back on your feet again. They are wonderful kids, and I know from my relationship with Nana and Pop-Pop that grandparents can be a grounding force in a child's life—and I know my parents love them dearly. But spending quality time together is not the same thing as being raised by them. My sister got offered a second chance to be carefree and single and she jumped at it.

The codependency demon didn't just grab hold of my sister. It took me years of pain, struggle and therapy to realize the patterns and dysfunction of my childhood created a perfect codependent storm of my own, especially in my relationships. And who would imagine someone who talks in front of thousands of people at a time and appears on television would have moments of crippling anxiety? And then there's depression. I know I am sooo not alone in this—so many of us battle these debilitating conditions daily. But I also know it's possible to feel better, and that's the main reason I am sharing my story now.

Looking at all of this, it begs the question: Where was my mother? She was at once a solid, loving force in my life while living completely under the control of my father. My best friend, she deserves her very own chapter, which appears at the end of this book.

CHAPTER 7

On The Rails

I wanted out. Out of Port Chester High School and out of Port Chester, period. I felt as if I were fleeing a fire. Graduation was like a rebirth to me—finally, I could do what I wanted, where I wanted, and without wondering if Mr. English was going to be waiting around every turn. My life was about to begin for real in every way. I felt like nothing could hold me back. I could make my own choices now. Decisions were now in my hands, and I was determined that I was going to be in control of my life from now on. I was able to see clearly how in high school I had created a full suit of emotional armor to fend off the bullying, the whispered rumors, and the direct insults. But I was now able to shed that armor and open up my soul to a lighter, brighter life. I was ready for the Big Apple!

Metro-North Railroad was my way of escaping Port Chester. In fact, I didn't wait to get to the city to escape. Every morning I took the train, not from the Port Chester station, but from the Rye station. I just felt like I needed a new start on every level, so my day began in Rye. I loved the train ride as well, watching my fellow commuters on their own journeys—listening to their conversations about their lives and jobs. While it's a relatively short train ride into Grand Central Terminal, I felt a bit like Harry Potter getting on the train to Hogwarts, emerging into an entirely different world than what I'd left. Stepping onto the platform and joining the throngs of people as we exited the station and scattered in a thousand different directions was exhilarating—and I was now a part of it! Grand Central Terminal is one of the most gorgeous places in New York and possibly the world. The grandeur of the Great Hall was like a metaphor for my new life: expansive, bustling, beautiful.

I had applied both to Hofstra University in Long Island and Fordham University in the Bronx. When I got accepted to Fordham, I decided immediately to attend their New York City campus near Lincoln Center. Now I could be in the middle of all of that city energy, instead of just getting the small taste when I was going down for auditions during high school. That first day on campus I was nervous, of course, but so excited. I followed the herd of students and tried to figure out what I was supposed to be doing! I knew no one but felt like I *did* know everyone, if that makes sense. All around were people like me! I let out the biggest sigh of my life—a sigh of relief and acceptance, finally.

Looking back, going to college in the city was probably more of a means to an end at that time than any driving desire I had to get a degree. Theater was in my blood from the many years I'd acted in school productions, and I thought THAT was really what I wanted to do. So, not only had I enrolled at Fordham, but I had also signed with an agency called Cuzzins Management, in an effort to pursue a career in acting. After I had my professional headshots taken, the agency sent them out for consideration for a number of roles—movies, commercials, plays. I didn't care where they wanted to hire me, I just wanted to be hired! I ended up being in a few TV commercials with national air play (including a Duncan Hines cookie spot); had a walk-on role in the soap *One Life to Live*; and was an extra in the movies *Fame* and *Pretty in Pink*.

It was exciting and fun . . . but when I was getting rejected for roles or commercials about 80 percent of the time, it really was a blow to my ego and confidence. I realized, even without being physically near me, Mr. English's influence was dragging me down again. For his own selfish reasons, he had filled my head with accolades about how amazing I was as an actor, given me lead roles that in reality should have gone to my talented fellow classmates, and basically set me up to think I was going to walk into a Broadway theatre or into a film studio and come away with a lead part. The fact was, I was a small fish in a very big pond of equally or more talented actors vying for the same roles I was. My conviction that NYC was where I was supposed to be was tested. I was second guessing my decision even before I really gave New York City a chance to either accept me or spit me out.

So, thank God for Fordham University – and Dan, someone who came into my life just when I needed him. He had a profound and lasting impact on me. We met two weeks after classes started and clicked immediately. I was standing in line for something and I felt a tap on my shoulder. Turning around, I saw a young man with dark hair and an average build, and he asked me where I was from.

"Port Chester," I replied. He shook his head in total non-recognition.

"Yeah," I said, "I try to forget I'm from there, too!"

Dan told me he was from Pittsburgh, which seemed just as foreign to me. Right off the bat, I could tell he was a nice guy. But something else too . . . I was pretty sure he was gay. That intrigued me and also made me a bit nervous because as I was starting to feel more comfortable in my own skin and space, I was beginning to notice handsome, creative, and interesting guys my age. Yet neither one of us mentioned our sexual orientation. We just simply became fast and fabulous friends.

It's a little sad but Dan was the first real, true friend I'd ever had. In fact, he really felt like a brother to me. He was confident and funny and we did everything together. We grabbed a hold of Manhattan and didn't let go— countless Broadway shows, dinners all over the island, and we'd even just hang out on campus or head up to the main Fordham Rose Hill campus in the Bronx, which is where Dan lived. I became friends with his friends up there.

It might surprise a lot of people to know making friends was hard for me then, and still is. Most people simply assume I am an extrovert, when the reality is I am a full-blown introvert. Shocker, right? For me it is easy to stand on stage and present to thousands, as well as be on TV . . . . but to step into a room of strangers or mingle at a party is painful and can stop me from being able to be fully present. I am often perceived as disengaged, not interested, and usually assumed to be full of myself. The reality is I am overly shy and lack confidence. Has that changed for me over the intervening years? A bit, yes, but it's still a daily challenge in my life, and I struggle with it and work hard to stand up to be seen and to be heard. The upside of being introverted is the innate empathy that goes hand in hand. I tend to see the best in others and try to help *them* step forward, find their voices, and really help them to be seen and heard. You can never go wrong being kind and respectful, and that awareness started with my friendship with Dan.

One day Dan asked me if I wanted to go out that night in Manhattan. I hesitated at the thought of going out and meeting strangers. He laughed it off and wouldn't take no for an answer. I don't recall exactly where we went, but the establishment was filled with happy, laughing people—mostly men, I noticed—having a great time. I never drank at all in high school, even when everyone else was getting wasted. I think it was a way for me to stay in control, at least of myself.

But that night I ordered a gin and tonic—my Nana's and Pop-Pop's drink of choice. It was the only thing I could think of to order! After we finished that, Dan ordered another round, then paused a beat, and said (didn't ask), "David, you DO know that you are gay, right?"

After years of being bullied, ridiculed, groomed by Mr. English, and called names by my peers, I had buried my sexuality for self-protection. I mean, my two sexual encounters up to that point had been *with women.* Plus, this was when HIV was ravaging the gay population, so I was petrified to have sex because I was sure I'd contract AIDS and die. (I know there was some holdover Catholic indoctrination in there too: enjoying unmarried sex will kill you!) But, finally, when this genuinely good guy, who was openly gay, yet had no agenda except to be my friend, opened the door for me, I hesitated, thinking to myself, "*Oh God, Oh God, this is happening now!*" I paused, breathed deeply to calm my nerves, and for the first time in my life said, "Yes, I AM gay!" I had never uttered the word "gay" about myself up to that point. The liberation and relief I felt was physical.

I was and still am so grateful for the way Dan outed me—slow, kind, and without drama. We had the most fun that year, even venturing to gay clubs and bars. Dan showed me that being gay was not scary or bad or the "death sentence" I came to think it was based on the behavior of Mr. English. Nor did it need to be secretive. Dan really helped me build my confidence as a young gay adult. Being gay finally just felt normal; no stress, no whispers, and no drama! I was just being myself, in my own skin and heart, every day, and feeling great about it.

I went to Pittsburgh to meet Dan's family, who were open and tolerant and sophisticated—just a completely different vibe than what I knew from Port Chester. His family even invited me to join them on vacation in Mexico, which was my first time out of the country. I was having the time of my life with a friend who wanted nothing from me except my friendship. No ulterior motives personally, emotionally, or sexually. Yet it was Dan who finally broke through and gave me permission to freely be who I really was.

Not only did I feel free to be me, I also found my voice to stand up for myself. The professor in my psychology class was completely homophobic. He said inappropriate and insulting things in class and even in the halls. And not just to me, but to other gay students as well. The old me would have seethed inside and let it go, but he did it one too many times, so I went to the grievance committee to complain about him. They were actually happy I made a formal complaint because they said they'd heard similar stories about him. He left shortly thereafter, and I know I had something to do with that. It was empowering, especially when my complaints about Mr. English had fallen on deaf ears in high school.

During this time, I also started to take acting classes (to improve my skills and before I realized acting was not what I was meant to do), which is where I met Craig, who was eight years my senior. Craig was a seasoned actor, had been in movies and on Broadway, and was always so nice to me. He offered me a place to stay when we had late classes, and there were no strings attached. Actually, I never asked nor wondered or cared if he was straight or gay. At Craig's, I slept on the sofa; he was lonely in the city and was just being a good person.

I was still carrying with me the worry about sex, and the suspicion about others' ulterior motives, which had been instilled in me by Mr. English. He had created the expectation in my mind that everyone wants something in return (how ironic coming from him). Thing is, I was never really able to shake that assumption, and as I gained celebrity status—such an awkward and cold way to be defined—I sadly realized there are a lot of people who really DO want something from you. If you have something that they think will bring them success and power, they are on you like flies on honey. It's an unfortunate part of being successful in the entertainment industry, and I have never been comfortable with it. Being referred to as a "celebrity" or a "talent" has always rubbed me the wrong way, and I want only to be known as me—someone who works hard to achieve my own version of success.

On the nights I decided to stay in the city, I would call home to my parents and let them know I wouldn't be home that night. They never asked where I was or who I was with. Were they curious at all? I never got "the talk" from my father, but looking back now, I'm not sure he'd know what to say to a young gay man (and I know deep inside he knew, even if he didn't want to admit it). He just left it to me to figure it out for myself. And I did. But as a parent now, I ask every question under the sun to make sure I feel comfortable and assured my children are safe.

People really do come into your life for a reason, a season, or for lifetime. Dan absolutely entered mine for a reason—the best reason ever, because if not for his friendship, I don't know how long it would have taken me to embrace myself completely, without shame or confusion or trepidation. He literally helped me step into the person I was meant to be. But as it turned out, Dan was also in my life for only a season, because after a year and a half at Fordham, I decided to leave school. As it happens, when we take a different path, friendships and people fade away when we don't see them every day. But I think of Dan often and have wanted to say how grateful I am for the healthy, kind, caring, important—albeit short—friendship we shared.

Attending college was never something I was eager or driven to do   it was simply the most natural way to escape Port Chester, even it was just for the school day or while I was pursuing other activities. And acting wasn't working out like I'd hoped. I was getting tired of rejections and feeling a bit lost in my life. Having no money made it even harder. I didn't want to leave my friends in the city, but I started to think this journey was not for me. I had the urge to work, to make money, and to find a way to really start something—something that would help me create and mold a career, something I would be in charge of. So, as much as I loved being in New York City, I sure as hell couldn't afford to live there. Sometimes, if the conditions are right, the quicksand you once were stuck in feels safe to test again. And for me, that decision was to return to Port Chester to live full time while continuing to attend Fordham. And, yes, that meant moving back into my parents' home—but only until I could afford a place of my own.

During that first summer between my freshman and sophomore year, I answered an ad in the newspaper looking for someone to deliver singing telegrams. You know how you can look back and pinpoint the EXACT moment in your life that led to everything else in your life? For me, it was taking that job with Witty Ditty in Scarsdale, New York, a very wealthy town about half way between Port Chester and New York City. Of course, I didn't know that at the time, only that it was really good money for a college kid! And it was a blast. The wonderful look on the person's face when I started singing, balloons in hand, and, more often than not, wearing some ridiculous costume, was worth as much as the money to me. And it also meant I WASN'T working at the funeral home!

Since I had to actually write the ditties I sang based on the person and the event that was being celebrated, I got to express my creativity as well. And the years of performing in musicals in high school certainly helped. On a more practical note, I actually had to find my way to wherever I had to be. I had rarely driven outside Port Chester up until then, and, mind you, this was before Waze and Google Maps, so the front of my white van was strewn with paper maps, tangles of balloons, which often floated into the passenger's seat, and I was frequently wearing a chicken or gorilla costume, and . . . well, you get the idea.

I had the requisite barbershop quartet outfit and a gold lamé tux (*A Chorus Line* was still a hit on Broadway) as well as a few other less cumbersome costumes I wore to deliver the telegrams. But the craziest things seemed to happen when I was dressed like a chicken or gorilla. The former getup included a big feathery yellow body, huge chicken feet and hands (okay, chickens don't have hands, but I had to hold the balloons and drive!), and, of course, a chicken headpiece, complete with a beak and a cock's comb.

One time I was driving on busy Central Avenue in Yonkers on my way to a gig when I rear-ended the car in front of me. The young woman emerged from her car and I got out as well. She took one look at me in my chicken costume and she jumped back into her car and sped off! Pretty sure she took me for some sort of nut and figured any ding in her bumper wasn't worth tangling with a huge chicken! I didn't always have my costume on in the car, but the time I decided to put it on right before my engagement, I managed to drop my keys into a sewer grate as well as one of my chicken feet! So, the folks on Greenwich Avenue that day were serenaded by a one-footed chicken who then had to call for a ride back home, where thankfully there was an extra set of keys.

My gorilla costume saw some action, too. I was speeding to get to a house party to sing my ditty and got pulled over by a local cop. I scared the hell out of him when he leaned down to ask for my license and registration! Then he started laughing hysterically when I explained myself and told me to get on my way, just a little bit slower.

The joke was on me the time I showed up at the address provided and found out I had been pranked when a bunch of "adult" kids started chasing me around the property. I don't recommend trying to run fast in a gorilla suit!

Of course, it wasn't always the costume that created a stir. Once on Long Island, I pulled into a gas station that was situated on a median. I got out to ask for directions but neglected to put the car in "Park," and it proceeded to roll away and crash into another car. Imagine explaining to your insurance company how your driverless car got into an accident with another driverless car.

I'd been working for Witty Ditty for about six months, and we just seemed to be getting ever busier. One day the owner, Emily, asked me if I wanted to buy the business! She and her husband were moving to Florida and making a clean break. Keep in mind, I was only nineteen at the time. The chance to own my own business was the last thing I had expected. The only problem was the $12,000 that she wanted for it. No way did I have that kind of money nor did my parents (and I'm not confident my father would have loaned it to me if he had). But Pop-Pop came to the rescue. Not only did he give me the loan, but he sat me down and gave me the speed-reading version of business school. All those years of owning his own successful florist shop imbued him with a depth of knowledge that he happily passed on to me. It felt a bit like he was passing on his legacy. And I absorbed every detail. This was such an exciting opportunity for me (of course I had NO idea where it would eventually lead), but it meant I had a big decision to make as well: college or my own business. I decided to pour myself headlong into Witty Ditty. And I have never, ever regretted that decision.

For the first year, I ran my business out of my bedroom back home, storing supplies in the garage. Not optimal, but I made the best of it. Business continued to get better, and I knew I had to get out of my parents' home and into a storefront. I found the perfect little place in Larchmont, New York—a 600-square-foot space right next to the movie theatre. That locale probably did as much for my business as anything, with all those people queuing up several times a day and night, waiting to get into the theater and peeking into my storefront. I stuck a table in the front window and each month decorated it with a different theme. One month I draped it in gold lamé and black fabric adorned with black and gold ostrich feathers. It was eye-catching for sure! And it caught the eye of Harriet, a woman who popped into the store after her movie was over. She asked me to decorate her son Seth's bar mitzvah. I had no idea what a bar mitzvah was, but that didn't stop me from giving her an enthusiastic "Yes!" Crazy, I know, but Port Chester was overwhelmingly Catholic when I was thirteen and evading the jerks in middle school, so I had no Jewish friends who might have invited me to a bar mitzvah. But I did have some Jewish friends at nineteen, so I called one of them and asked him to walk me through this ritual into adulthood.

And so it began. Word of mouth is absolutely priceless, and that's how I became the king of decorating bar and bat mitzvahs in Westchester County and Long Island. Believe it or not, I also started getting hired to decorate for *brit milah,* or bris, ceremonies as well, where baby boys are circumcised too much celebrating and fanfare. (Always wondered: Did they hire me first or the mohel who did the snipping?) And then came the weddings . . .

My life and work during that time was creating parties for the Jewish community in Westchester. I have to credit my Jewish friends and clientele back then for helping me really get my business off the ground. They welcomed me and gave me a great education. Finally, this Italian-Catholic boy from Port Chester learned about the *tallit* (the prayer shawl), the *chuppah* (the traditional canopy under which the bride and groom stand), the *hamotzi,* the blessing of the bread, the *Mizinke* dance at weddings . . . and the list goes on. These wonderful people taught me everything I needed to know about being the best decorator for any celebration. And it wasn't just about Jewish traditions.

Given the fact that an enormous part of my career has been centered around wedding planning, having written books and hosted TV shows about it, you might be surprised at how much I *didn't* know when I first got started. Charger plates? I had no idea these existed. Formal place settings? I quickly had to learn the layout for flatware, silverware, and glassware. And two tablecloths? Why did you need two for one table? Oh . . . the underlay and overlay. Got it. And the first time someone asked me about chair covers, I silently asked myself why would we need to cover the chairs? To make them prettier and to create a coordinated look, of course. Then there was the difference between escort cards and place cards: the former tells a guest which table they can sit at while the latter tells them the *exact* seat where they will sit—subtle but important differences, depending upon how formal a wedding it is.

Very few of us land on our feet right away, personally or professionally. Some people influence us negatively, and some are the guiding lights to get us on the path to happiness and success. Dan. Harriet. Pop-Pop. The entire Jewish community of Westchester who gave me my start. I am so grateful for every one of them.

CHAPTER 8
Off the Rails

Never say never, right? Port Chester was the last place I thought I'd return to—but being there on my own terms and running my own business made a world of difference. In the two years since I'd graduated high school, I felt like I had uncovered my authentic self, found my voice, and knew I'd never take shit from anyone ever again. Little did I know. At only twenty, I, of course, still had a lot to learn about a lot of things. But we often don't know what we need to know without knocks upside the head.

It all started with an invitation to a barbecue in Bronxville, New York. A female friend of mine asked me to come with her. Irony of ironies, this future party planner finds it painful to attend a party. Behind the scenes and making sure everyone else has a great time is one thing, but mingling and making small talk with strangers is so terribly hard for me—even more so back then.

I was standing around, holding a red Solo cup of beer to look like I belonged (even though I hate beer), and I noticed these two guys standing across the yard by a tree. Both were very handsome. The taller of the two, whom I found out later was Frank, had on a tight tank top and short shorts. He was stunning and as handsome as a model. The other man, Michael, was shorter, darker, very animated, and full of energy (something I would come to find out was likely chemically augmented). It seemed obvious to me that they were a couple, yet Michael, the life of the party, began to stare at me.

When Frank walked into the house, Michael came over to me, told me he thought I was cute, and asked me out on a date. No small talk or beating around the bush.

Taken aback, I stammered, "But what about him?" gesturing toward the house.

"Frank doesn't need to know," he replied. He slipped me his number and told me to call before walking away.

After that encounter, the rest of the barbecue was a bit of a blur. In the category of hindsight is 20/20, I should have chucked his number into the trash along with the Solo cup. But I was too young, too flattered, and too attracted to do the smart thing. And the right thing, since it was clear Michael already had a boyfriend. He wasn't really my type, but I was thrilled by the attention.

After a few days went by, I couldn't help myself. I swallowed my morals and called Michael, unwittingly starting a rollercoaster ride I didn't know how to get off of. We met for dinner, and I was immediately infatuated. He was smart, funny, kind, and had an engaging personality. For an introvert like me, Michael was the yang to my yin, which made me believe we were meant for each other. Despite the fact he was still with Frank, Michael and I started dating regularly, and before long, I was completely head over heels in love.

Frankly, I was lost and looking for home—not just a physical home but an emotional and spiritual one, too. I've been called a "fairy godfather" by clients and colleagues appreciative of how I make their dream weddings or celebrations come true for them. I'm honored and flattered by the title, but at the time, it was *me* who was looking for a fairy godfather or godmother to guide me. I was definitely *not* the buttoned-up, happy, positive person people would later see on TV. Searching for love and happiness was exactly what I was trying to do, but I went about it in a way that frequently and ironically brought about the opposite result.

Maybe it was all those years performing in musicals in school, but I often had a soundtrack playing in my head and one song in particular seemed to be on repeat (any parent with daughters addicted to *Frozen* will completely relate!). The song that so resonated with me was from *The Wiz*, that remake of *The Wizard of Oz* with a marvelous all-Black, all-star cast that included Michael Jackson, Richard Pryor, Nipsy Russell, and, of course, Diana Ross. "There's no place like home," says Dorothy. And I realized that's what I had been missing, so it was Diana-as-Dorothy's final song, "Home," that felt like it was written just for me.

This chapter of my life was me going off the rails, pushing away the pain and forgetting my past and just trying to have fun and finding myself. I was looking for a re-do, an escape, a new beginning that only I controlled, without realizing that I was actually stepping into a very dark place. Mr. English's years of grooming and the AP Literature teacher "competing" to have sex with me my senior year, coupled with the lack of guidance and concern by the adults in charge . . . it was almost as if Michael had been waiting for me to arrive to lead me even further into darkness.

I never knew if it was because of me, but a few months after I started up with Michael, he and Frank had a huge fight, and Frank was out of the picture. Our relationship picked up speed, and after a while Michael invited me to start staying over a few nights a week at his cottage in Purchase, only about two-and-a-half miles from my parents' house. I was ecstatic. Not only would I be with my boyfriend (my very first!), but it also meant I wouldn't be under the same roof with my father. Michael was a professional dog handler (think Westminster Kennel Club) and groomer, and ran his company out of his home. (As an aside, *that* is an odd, almost cult-like group of people—the dog show set. If you haven't seen the movie *Best In Show*, check it out because it's spot on.)

After spending enough nights at Michael's, I got to meet more of his friends and was introduced to a lifestyle completely alien to me. Namely, they were majorly into cocaine. And it was available all the time. It was like dating Halston without the glamour and the money! As I mentioned before, I never drank or even smoked pot in high school, and only starting enjoying cocktails in college with Dan. After a while, I guess I got so used to the coke being around and Michael and everyone partaking, that I decided to give it a try. And . . . I liked it. For the first time in my life, I felt like an extrovert since it completely dissolved my inhibitions. I know that wasn't the real me, but it did feel good being someone else for a change.

This was an exhilarating time in my life. I was running my own business, was in love, and had someone who loved me. Or so I believed. Did I mention that Michael was fifteen years older than me? It wasn't like he was a father figure (though I could see how I might be looking even subconsciously for one given my relationship with my father), but he did like to take care of me, look after me, and genuinely seemed to adore me. After a few months, Michael asked me to move in with him permanently and announced he'd found a great apartment for us . . . wait for it . . . in Port Chester! Fucking Port Chester was like a vortex I'd never be able to escape. But I was desperate to get out of my parents' home for good, even though by that time I came and went as I pleased, no questions asked. Moving in with my boyfriend felt right, and so I said yes, Port Chester or not.

I remember telling my mother that I was moving out. I came downstairs to find her at the sink, washing dishes. "Mom," I said calmly. "I am moving out this week and moving in with my boyfriend, Michael. And Mom, I'm gay. I found a few books that I think might be helpful for you and Dad. And I'm very open to talking about anything you want."

My mom said, "Thank you," then uncharacteristically forceful for her, added, "NEVER share any of this with your father. Ever!" And THAT was the only time we ever talked about my sexuality. She accepted me, loved me, but I knew then for sure I'd never be accepted by my father.

And so I moved in with Michael. For a while it was great. We had lots of fun, lots of great dinners and vacations and, yes, lots of sex. Michael loved sex. I had managed to conquer the fear of sex I'd had because of the HIV epidemic because if we were monogamous, what was there to worry about?

Aside from sex, Michael loved cocaine. In fact, the two became so inter-twined that he reached a point where he was only able to perform if he'd snorted coke. Looking back now, I can see clearly what I didn't see then: he was an addict (of both drugs and sex), and I was codependent, believing my love for him meant doing whatever made him happy.

Then the mood swings and fighting started. He would go from telling me how much he loved me to screaming at me and then apologize. He would turn aggressive and angry in an instant, without warning. My head and heart were spinning. The fights turned violent, and Michael would punch me in the face, pull my hair, and even once threw me out of the apartment one night. But I still thought I could help him if I stayed and tried to get him help. That is the tragic, vicious truth of codependency—erroneously thinking that YOU have any control whatsoever over the situation. But addiction—to drugs, alcohol, sex, whatever—was stronger than either one of us.

Anyone who has lived with an addict knows how hard it can be to leave, because deep down there is still this hope that love will conquer all. But not without help, and not without the addict admitting he needs help. I'd love to say I left after the first time (or second or third time) he got violent, but I didn't. Instead, I essentially became Michael's babysitter. I remember coming home from work more than once to find him in either a pool of blood or his own piss, his face smashed up after a night on the town, and no memory of it whatsoever. Or the times he could hold himself together long enough to accompany me and friends on a dinner date, only to have him start to fall apart halfway through—and I'd grab the check and try to get him out before he caused a real scene. The trips where I'd walk him off airplanes after he'd overindulged in booze (or coke in the bathroom) on the flight, trying to get him out of there fast and out of harm's way. Or the time he crashed our car and left it along the side of the road, only to tell me the next day that someone had stolen it. His lies to mask the truth or his memory blackouts became more and more pathetic.

One evening the doorbell of our apartment rang, and I opened the door to a strange man who walked in and gave Michael an enormous white rock, for which Michael then handed him thousands of dollars in cash. I was dumbstruck and had no idea what was going on. "You fucking idiot," Michael screamed at me. "It's coke! Fucking coke! Now get over here and do some with me."

Which I now knew meant he'd want to have sex later. What had started as so loving became something I feared . . . again. I was truly becoming scared for my own mental and physical health, with good reason, as it turned out.

I should have realized that his sexual addiction was just as bad as his drug addiction, which meant he'd find it whenever, wherever, and with whomever. I discovered he was going to gay bathhouses, meeting strangers in rest areas along the highway, answering classified ads. OMG, I realized, he was just like Mr. English! I also found out Michael was going to orgies! Even worse (what's worse than an orgy?!), he told me he was going to have unprotected sex with his friend Mark, who had contracted AIDS, because he felt bad for him, and was starting to fall in love with Mark.

Finally, that was my breaking point. I told Michael I was leaving him, and he attacked me—it was the most scary and dangerous night ever. He didn't believe me, but as soon as he stormed out to God knows where and with whom, I packed one suitcase, and called my Aunt Maria to come get me.

My aunt, whom I've called RiRi from the time I was small, was more of a sister to me than an aunt. My mom's younger sister by nearly fifteen years, it was as if Nana and Pop-Pop had raised two only children. And they could hardly have been more different, though each of them inherited my nana's kindness and big caring heart. Where my mother worked briefly before getting married and raising three kids, RiRi began to pursue her love of theatre and singing immediately after graduating high school. After that, she got her nursing degree. RiRi was my bright light in many times of darkness. And that night I left Michael was one of the darkest. She took me in, and, instead of chastising me I for staying with him for so long, gently suggested that I should go to an Al-Anon meeting. She always guided, never pushed. That it took me many more years, after a relationship with another addict, to follow her advice was no fault of hers.

RiRi kept an apartment in Greenwich Village and let me stay there often. She took me to restaurants and jazz clubs (her first husband was a well-known jazz musician), which whetted my appetite for NYC. While she never had children of her own, she has brought thousands into the world as a certified nurse midwife and has been a professor at Columbia University School of Nursing for decades. Our daughters adore her. In fact, she flew to Kansas with my mother to help me bring Cielo home and get me settled in as a new father. Over the years, we have traveled to Paris and Italy together. Coming full circle, RiRi is once again singing cabaret in New York City. A beacon of light, love, and kindness, she has been my muse. Without her and my mom's guidance and love, I truly do not know how I would have survived.

That night RiRi took me in. I never returned or saw or spoke to Michael again. But a year and a half later, I heard about him from the most unexpected source: my father.

"David," he said over the phone. "I have a death call I thought you might want to know about. Your friend Michael. . . ." (He knew he had been my boyfriend but refused, even now, to call him that.) "He overdosed and is dead and is here at the funeral home with me." No empathy, no sympathy, or easing into the news gently. I think my father's delivery was almost as shocking and painful as the news itself. I can't even remember if I responded to my father before hanging up. Then I just lost it, sobbing. I was devastated.

Michael was very fucked up, abusive, and struggled with many demons, but that doesn't take away the fact that I loved him. I did what I needed to do to save myself—mind, body, and soul—and survive the heartache and chaos. I did attend his wake (at my father's funeral home) and honored the love I had for him and remembered the good man that was overtaken by his addictions.

I think this was the final push for me to get out of Port Chester. I moved in with my Aunt Maria for a bit and then found my very first solo apartment in White Plains. Maybe it was only eight miles from my home town, but it felt like a million miles and a lifetime away. I finally did it—I left Port Chester, and I never, ever lived there again.

Sharing this part of my life was a hard decision, knowing I am making myself a target for judgment or shaming. But in the end, I realized that everything I've been through, dark or light, made me who I am. Life shifts and moves and sometimes cracks all the way open, dropping us into an abyss that some never crawl back out of. This time in my life that started with Michael was the beginning of a very long, curving road with a hell of a lot of potholes as well as some open road with the wind in my hair. And I took a lot of detours and wrong turns with no one to blame but myself. And that's the point—each of us travels our own road, and there is absolutely nothing to be ashamed of when that road gets rocky.

CHAPTER 9

The Blow Up

B y now it's hopefully clear that my father is a control freak—capital C, Capital FREAK. One aspect of that is he is also a clean fanatic, to put it mildly. He is and has always been obsessed with germs. I mean, he has led his life assuming he was under attack by germs—that they were personally out to get him. I'm sure his germophobia had everything to do with his work, moving dead bodies, and all the ministrations he performs once he gets them back to the funeral home. Blood, fecal matter, and any other disgusting matter he has to handle in his job. And even though *we* didn't have to deal with this stuff, we certainly had to hear about it every day when he got home. I know most people need to decompress and talk shop a bit after a long day, but the stuff he talked about should never be a topic of conversation, ever, with anyone.

His work also put him in a lot of hospitals and nursing homes as well, so his obsession with cleanliness is understandable. But there's clean, and there's neurotically clean. And then there's pushing that neurosis onto your kids. My father was using Windex on everything long before we saw it in the movie *My Big Fat Greek Wedding*! Added to his arsenal were Lysol spray, antibacterial wipes, and, of course, latex gloves.

From my earliest childhood, I remember him telling my siblings and me exactly how to do everything to avoid touching a single, solitary germ (which, of course, is completely impossible). "Don't touch the handrail on the escalator!" What?? So I learned to lean with my forearm on the rail, which was a bit of a balancing act, especially if my hands were full of purchases.

"Don't touch the buttons on the elevator!" Seriously? He showed us how to pull our sleeves over our fingers to push the buttons, which, of course, only worked if we were wearing long sleeves. In the event I just had on a T-shirt, I was to stick my hand under the hem of my shirt to cover my button-pushing finger. To say we looked like lunatics is an understatement.

And the pièce de résistance? Public Bathroom Choreography. My father was adamant that we not touch anything anywhere in a bathroom. Nothing. *Then how in the hell are we supposed to go?* I remember thinking. My father's instructions were as follows: Use only a foot to open the door to the restroom or, if it opens outward, the ol' sleeve-or-shirt-hem-over-your-hand trick. Open the stall door with a hip or covered arm. Flush toilet with a foot, pull stall door open with foot or, again, fabric-covered hand. Washing hands was a ballet all its own: Grab paper towels to turn on the faucet (this was well before motion-sensor faucets), stand at least six inches away from the sink, and lean over to wash hands for AT LEAST one full minute. Then, of course, turn off the faucet with more paper towels. Don't touch the walls, don't touch the doors, don't touch anything, and, if we could, avoid breathing!

Okay, so I want to thank my father for teaching us how to protect ourselves from germs and to stay as clean and healthy as possible. Basically, my father was prepared for COVID decades before it arrived. But when it did, he was masked, gloved, and had his germophobe tool kit at the ready, hazmatted up to live his germ-free life to the fullest!

While my father's clean-freakism was incredibly neurotic and annoying, he truly did mean it as a way to protect himself and us. Which is why this next story takes the prize for irony—the one about how my father blew up our house.

I was working at my office in Mamaroneck, New York, and got a phone call from a woman who worked with my mother at the time in the nurse's office at the high school.

"Your parents' house is on fire! *Get there right away!*"

Fire is always alarming, but I still figured it was just some small thing. This was before cell phones, so there was no way for me to reach any of my family to see what the hell was going on. I jumped in my car and sped up the Hutchinson River Parkway to Port Chester.

It was like the set of a movie! Fire trucks and police everywhere. People standing on the lawns of the houses across the street, which, since they were on a slight incline, provided a perfect view of what used to be my house. It wasn't just on fire—it was burned to the ground! By the time I arrived, my father was on a stretcher with burns on one arm and from his chest to his waist.

What the hell had happened? I was thinking a natural gas explosion or perhaps a meth lab in our basement that I wasn't aware of. By the time I made my way over to my father, he was out of it. Kept asking me to go into the kitchen (no kitchen left) and grab his wallet that was in the pocket of his jacket hanging over the back of a chair (no chair left, no jacket left, and no wallet left). That's how out of it he was, that he didn't realize there was nothing left to go back into the house to retrieve. Even as he was being loaded into the back of the ambulance, he was instructing me to go upstairs (what stairs?) and get all of the important papers on his dresser. "And your mother's jewelry!" It was only the fact that the EMTs closed the ambulance doors that I didn't hear any more impossible-to-follow orders, but I'm sure he was still giving them all the way to the hospital.

Perhaps because my father was well-known in the community, one of the firemen who overheard my father giving me instructions wanted him to know that at least they *tried* to recover something from the ruins. So, he gave me a pair of boots and the pants with the proverbial suspenders, then a fireman's coat. Finally, he popped a helmet on my head and led me into the smoldering house. Of course, it was futile. There truly was nothing left to retrieve. It was all just ashes.

Outside, I found my mother, brother, and sister sitting among the spectators, all in shock. What's incredible is that my siblings and their dog, Corey, had been in the house but managed to escape. And I would discover that this poor innocent dog was unwittingly the cause of this catastrophe.

Corey was an Old English Sheepdog. Way too much dog for a 1,600-square-foot house. So, apparently Corey had an accident. And being a big dog, it was a sizable one. He pooped on the floor in the small room off the laundry room. Shit happens, right? Most people would yell at the dog, clean it up, and go about their day. Not my father. He did clean the spot on the carpet but didn't stop there. He then pulled up the carpet and started to clean the tiles UNDER the carpet—specifically, he tried to remove the glue from the tiles. It was a warm day, and he had the central air conditioning on as well (this is relevant, trust me). Because the glue had been there for years, it wasn't coming off easily. So, he tried various cleaning solutions, including turpentine and other noxious, fume-producing liquids, which, of course, got sucked into the rest of the house via the air conditioner ducts. When the solvents didn't do the trick on their own, he got a metal scraper (you see where this is going, right?) and went after the glue with that. And . . . the sparks he created with the scraper ignited the solvent fumes and literally blew up the house. That anyone survived this, especially my father, is a miracle.

The aftermath of this overzealous cleaning project was terrible for my family. My father was in the hospital for six months, recovering from his injuries. My mother, sister, and brother had to live at the Courtyard Marriott in neighboring Rye, New York, while the house was being rebuilt. I visited them often during this time and the tension was palpable. Even as easygoing as my mother and brother are, there's just so much togetherness in tight quarters, under such stress, that anyone can take.

The insurance on the house wasn't enough to cover the costs, so my father had to max out his credit cards and secure lines of credit to rebuild the house. And just to add another level of crazy to an already crazy situation, the contractor my father hired to rebuild the house was my ex-boyfriend Michael's brother! My father couldn't ever accept that I was gay or that Michael had been my boyfriend, but he had no problem hiring his brother. Truly, you can't make this stuff up.

And Corey? He was adopted by someone who had enough room for a dog like him. I believe he lived a better life after that—no more screaming, crazy man constantly washing everything down. I swear that if Corey stood in one place long enough, he'd have been sprayed with Lysol, scrubbed with bleach, and finished off with a Windex rinse.

CHAPTER 10
Burning the Candle at Both Ends

I may have escaped Michael and Port Chester—but I certainly didn't escape unscathed. Between the years of Mr. English and my relationship with Michael, I'd absorbed so much toxicity I felt like I should have worn a hazmat warning sign. When you are around situations or people that are poisonous, it seeps into your soul and heart and brain, and you don't even realize it. You do what you can to survive, but it takes its toll. You may still know right from wrong, but you lose perspective.

A lot of kids who never partied in high school end up going nuts during that first year of freedom in college—getting drunk or high, just going crazy because they can. It's as if a giant escape valve has been released. After Michael died, that was me. It was as if all the rage, fear, shame, sadness, anxiety, and every other negative emotion you can name reached a boiling point, and, if I didn't release it, it would burn me alive. I'm not proud of those days, but they shaped me and helped me become the person I am today.

I had been a scared, bullied kid on the playground in school, but now it was *my* time to play on my terms, and my terms only. So, I went back to the playground where I'd enjoyed myself: New York City. Sometimes I'd just drive in by myself to hang out and party and people watch.

It was on one of these trips that I met Robbie, a straight and recently divorced doctor, who quickly became a close friend. He was well-traveled, funny, and from a well-off Jewish family. We went to clubs all of the time and went a little bit crazy. Monday nights we'd hit a gay club, Wednesday nights a straight club, and, finally, on the weekend, a totally over-the-top gay club. I had the biggest boy crush on Robbie, but it was purely plutonic, just flirtation and fun. I think we were both curious about the "other side," but we stayed in our own lanes, so to speak. He also introduced me to the world. I traveled to Paris with him (my first trip to Europe), and we had the time of our lives, partying at the Buddha-Bar and (my favorite) Le Queen, which put the gay in "Gay Par-ee"—it was out of control. Robbie really opened my eyes to a bigger picture of life. Thank you, Robbie, for being that friend right when I needed one, for making me smile and laugh and for being my partner in crime, figuratively speaking (although I do recall getting caught in a bathroom stall doing coke at the Roxy and being kicked out. Then I sneaked back in to rejoin Robbie!).

Going out to party was my escape, where I felt happiness and freedom. I can recall my times on the dance floor—at the Roxy, the Private Eyes, the Sound Factory, and even Studio 54—as ones of pure joy. I loved sitting in the balcony at the Palladium, stoned and immersing myself in the music and lights . . . and sights. There was always a "show" going on—people making out or even having sex. My favorite moments were being in the center of the dance floor alone, dancing and looking up at the colored lights and the confetti in the air, moving to the thumping bass of the music. Seeing the smiles on strangers' faces. Once I even looked over and saw Madonna doing the same thing as me—dancing her life away and loving every minute. While I had fun and made out a lot, I never got involved sexually with anyone during that time. Remembering Mr. English's positive HIV diagnosis and Michael's rampant cheating (even *knowingly* with HIV-positive men!), I was now truly scared to death of sex. Again. I equated it with something dirty. Sex was the enemy and a death sentence. It was an extreme response to what happened with Michael, but looking back it probably wasn't the worst time to be celibate in New York City.

But what I lacked in sex, I made up for in other ways. Shockingly (not), I was introduced to the world of drugs beyond the cocaine that I had shared with Michael and his crowd. I was around a lot of people with money, which meant drugs were always available in abundance and variety. I became close to a well-known writer as well as celebrities and TV personalities and fashion designers. Clearly, there was no shortage of free chemical entertainment. In my mid- twenties, my career as an event and wedding planner was really taking off, but I still needed so much to be a part of that NYC energy and insanity. Of course, one very perilous side effect of taking drugs is that they can make you feel invincible and capable of anything. I admit that happened to me. I was still in the throes of my I'll-do-what-I-fucking-well-please period, but even then, in the back of my mind, I knew building my career and this lifestyle were ultimately incompatible. But I wasn't ready to stop yet. I finally felt free, unafraid, outgoing, and *not* lost. I look back and see now I made some very foolish choices, but at that time, the only thing that mattered was they were *my* choices.

Robbie introduced me to quaaludes and I was like "Thank you, Robbie!" I loved how free and open I felt. Considering they are downers, I am shocked how alive they made me feel. Perhaps I liked how they took the edge off my anxiety. Then another friend, Laura, *re*introduced me to cocaine. I had (wisely) avoided it up to that time as I associated it with the trauma of my relationship with Michael, and how coke had played such an integral role in all of that. But I decided to give it another try, I mean *everyone* was doing it. Cocaine gave me unending energy, and I could stay up for days at a time it seemed—I got so much done! And no longer did I have to wait for the next party or event because soon I had my own dealer, Frenchie Phillip. He was but a phone call away. We'd meet on a NYC street corner, where he'd hand off an envelope filled with coke.

And next came Ecstasy . . . and to me that name was exactly what I felt when I took it. Ecstasy became my new best friend. Coupled with a hit or two of coke, I was good to go all night on the dance floor; all inhibitions and fears completely vanished. It totally allowed me to live in the moment, which felt incredible *in the moment*. In my sober hours, however, I began to admit that burning the candle at both ends was not only exhausting, but it curtailed my ability to be creative. I had reached a turning point.

What I didn't realize is just how *long* I had been burning that candle. After seven years of that crazy life of late, drug-fueled nights (i.e., little sleep), balanced by different drugs in the morning to fuel my day, I realized if I was going to truly make something of myself, I had to jump off the crazy train and devote myself completely—and soberly—to my career. My days (or mostly nights) of extreme play in NYC had to come to a stop. During this time, I became very well-known as an event planner and designer in the city and surrounding communities. Business was increasing, clients were becoming more demanding, and things were really taking off. Had I not fully pulled myself together right then, it would have been a tipping point for my career, and not a good one. I am confident there never would have been any TV shows, books, product lines, wedding fashions, or *anything* with my name attached, except maybe a toe tag if I kept up my full-tilt life.

Instead, this was the point when things started getting better and better *because* I stopped. I knew I wasn't chemically addicted—but I was emotionally. And when I embraced the fact that I *loved* my job and wanted to take it as far as I possibly could, I realized that I was finally *ready* to stop. My career needed my full, clear-headed attention. Burning the candle at both ends had its time and place and was a part of my life I wouldn't trade for anything (though I might have shaved a few years off in hindsight!). At the time, I was carrying too much pain and I needed to just feel good.

I discovered, finally, that pain can be power. When you can harness your pain, direct it appropriately and with passion, your struggles can turn into success. Pain is part of who we are and it's important to honor it for its place in our lives—but we are not meant to live with it forever. You can turn it around to become light and love and strength once you start to really take care of yourself first (and that includes following your dreams). I read somewhere "You can only love someone as much as you love yourself." And I didn't love myself or treat myself very well up at that time. But burning that candle, pardon the expression, showed me the light. Only when my life became so polarized did I see that my determination to control my life the way I wanted was temporarily blinding me to the possibility that I was, ironically, in danger of losing control over the one thing that really mattered to me: my future.

It's been many years since those party days and leaving the drugs bchind. My highs now come from my two amazing daughters and my husband, Joey. And also from helping others realize their dreams. I'm living the life I wanted for so long.

CHAPTER 11
Billionaire Bitches

Some people are just born nice. And some people . . . aren't. Add a billion or so dollars to the latter and Oh. My. God. Look out. Oddly enough, while I have worked for some absolutely lovely people in my career (some rich, some far from it), it was the billionaire bullies that taught me the most. Having grown up bullied, I was tough as nails and could handle anything they threw at me. And some of them had a really good arm!

These were the wives of heads of some of the largest financial institutions in the world—the "better half" of men who owned hotel chains and professional sports teams. Some of them had personal art collections to rival many galleries or museums. In other words, these were not the people I grew up with.

These women (and yes, they were all women) made demands to which "no" or even "maybe" was simply not an option. They could hurl insults at me one minute and then tell me in the next breath how I was now one of the family! (I already had one dysfunctional family, thank you very much!) Frankly, they scared the shit out of me, and at the same time they were instrumental in building my career. In fact, many reminded me that creating a party for them would change my life! And they were right. They helped me discover and grow talent I didn't even know I had, and I thank them from the bottom of my heart for that. By the way, billionaires stay billionaires because they know how to bargain (most of them bargained me down!), so I also learned the delicate art of negotiating.

These, ahem, lovely, kind, and caring women were my Professors of Party. Keep in mind, I grew up with parties that featured my mom's piñata, streamers, balloons, and an icebox cake with paper plates and napkins—and I wouldn't trade that for anything. But these ladies showed me how to up my game, taught me about etiquette, place settings and place cards, and about what was acceptable and what was not for their crowd. I learned fast because I listened and watched. Yet I never let on that in the beginning I was still a babe in the woods. You have to lead with confidence, and I acted like I already knew everything they taught me. The magic of fake it until you make it. It also helps to kill them with kindness. If I see potential disaster looming, I jump in and offer a compliment to shift the narrative: "I love your dress! Your hair is stunning that way! Or "You look radiant!" It always works, trust me. It won't last for long, but it gave me a moment to breathe and strategize.

The person—or should I say legend—who introduced me to this echelon of clients was the late grande dame of cake artistry, Sylvia Weinstock, who passed away in late 2021 at the age of ninety-one. Her over-the-top, beautiful creations that she decorated with life-like flowers were wanted by celebrities, politicians, and royalty. They were beyond parallel, and one of her cakes could run into the thousands. Sylvia was a retired teacher. She and her attorney husband, Ben, were two of the sweetest people you could ever know (no surprise her second career involved so much sugar!). My mom accompanied me at my first meeting with Sylvia when we drove down to her Tribeca home office and bakery. Later, I would meet Sylvia for dinner on occasion (she was also an amazing cook, or we would hit some restaurants in the city). She took a shine to me and said she wanted to help me get into the world of high-end events. I really had no idea how that would play out or ultimately change my life.

During this time, I also met a number of other event designers who catered to this exclusive crowd, and every one of them was arrogant, smug, and so full of themselves—always bragging about how wonderful and talented they were. Don't get me wrong—they were super-talented, but if they'd stepped off their pedestal and landed on the ground, they might have been kinder and nicer.

The first client Sylvia introduced me to was the inimitable Mrs. B., of Bel Air (and we'll get to her in a minute). The stories I share here are 100 percent true. No embellishments or exaggerations. As I wrote these memories down, I wondered how in the hell I withstood the insanity! And this is just a sampling – there are so many more. Fearing for my safety, I have only identified "my ladies" by their initials. (They'd kill me if I revealed their names!) But with grace I say, *thank you* to all the Ladies Who Lunch for giving me the path to follow, by showing me the bar for high expectations, and for teaching me that when I listened and worked hard, I learned. So for all the hell I had to put up with, it paid off. And *thank you* dear Sylvia for ushering me into this world.

Without further ado . . . here's to the Ladies Who Lunch, in no specific order because there's no way I could ever dare to play favorites!

• • ● ● ● • •

Mrs. B: Recently widowed, Mrs. B called my office in Mamaroneck, New York, telling me she had heard that I was someone she should consider to create her two (not one!) seventieth birthday celebrations. As she put it, "Night One is for my friends who are not special, and Night Two is for people so important it is imperative that none of the guests on either list know there are two parties to celebrate my birthday." Wow. Just knowing the names on these guest lists felt like having the secret nuclear codes!

I asked around and found out who her husband was—a billionaire who had left her the world, it seemed. They had just completed construction on what was at the time one of the largest homes in all of California. They had no children, and with Mr. B's passing, she was ready to celebrate life. She'd also inherited a large rare art collection. What she hadn't inherited was her husband's kindness—she was abrupt and demanding. Mrs. B was born in the Bronx and married her boss; you'd think she'd be a bit nicer to the "little folks," given her humble beginnings, but no.

I booked a coach ticket to L.A. and drove to her palatial residence in Bel Air in a roller skate of a rental car. I pulled up to the security booth (complete with armed guard) and waited to be admitted. Once inside this 85,000-square foot home with sixteen personal staff just for her (yes, you read that right), I was escorted to a second-floor waiting area. And there I sat, for an hour, with no idea of when I'd actually see her. Finally, a voice came over the PA system: "David Tutera, please meet with Mrs. B in dining room A in the Grand Hall."

Where the hell was the Grand Hall and how do I get there? No one came to escort me, and so I began to wander the mansion, sweating, and my nerves at an all-time high. It was like being in a lavish escape room! After a few futile minutes, I found a phone and was instantly greeted by, I presume, one of the sixteen staffers, asking how they might be of help. I told them I was lost and trying to find Mrs. B. And right away, a servant found me and led me to her, a frail-looking woman dressed to the nines and dripping with jewels in the middle of the afternoon.

She told me she loved flowers, wanted an overall look of opulence and French-inspired colors of lavender, yellow, and coral. She wanted a lovely combination of flowers, linens, place settings, and magnificent wine. And then she rose and began to walk out of the room, no good-bye, no follow-up instructions. This was *not* to be collaboration, sharing my ideas, and getting her reaction. I had my marching orders. But she did stop at the door, turned back to me, and said, "I know you are new to this level of entertaining, so price this LOW! I am not spending a lot!" Then she flew out on her broomstick!

Several weeks later, I got a frantic call from Mrs. B. "I must see the fabrics for the tablecloths and napkins immediately!"

I told her I could overnight the swatches and she cut me off in mid-sentence.

"That is unacceptable! I want you on the next flight out here to show them to me in person. Get out here or you are fired!"

I already knew I was losing money on this gig, but I had to view it as a loss leader, because I knew this was an opportunity that would open many other doors. So, I repeated the entire scenario from my first trip—from coach ticket to guard-booth gestapo to being deposited in a room to wait . . . and wait. . .and wait. Part of me wondered if there wasn't a hidden camera on me. When Mrs. B finally beckoned me, I was brought to her office to show her the linens. She took one look at me and said, "Why in the hell are you here?"

OMG, I thought. *Is she serious?*

She didn't even look at the fabrics and dismissed me, telling me she would call and let me know her selections.

And she did. And so a month later, I was back in L.A. to get down to the real work of planning her two birthday parties. Mrs. B's "humble abode" had two full catering kitchens, a full beauty salon, and an underground parking garage complete with fifteen Rolls-Royces, each one monitored by multiple video cameras. Her full-time hairdresser and chauffeur were on call 24/7.

I was given a workspace close to the parking garage. All I could afford was one floral assistant, but, like I said, I really needed to do this party to get on the radar of other big-money clients.

The morning of Party #1, Mrs. B got a bug in her ear to go get her hair done (then why have an in-house salon and hairdresser??) *and* she was going to drive herself (then why have a chauffeur?). The garage door opened, and Mrs. B, looking every bit the part of Cruella DeVil, came flying out in one of her Rolls-Royces, sped up the driveway, and sideswiped a wall, taking out the left side of her Rolls. I stood staring in shock! Then the car started to slowly reverse until it reached where I was standing, whereupon Cruella, or, I mean Mrs. B, rolled down her window and screamed at me that it was MY entire fault! She said I had blocked her line of sight, and I would be held fully responsible for the repairs to her car. Then she sped away like a bat out of hell (how appropriate).

I was stunned. There was no way I could pay to repair a Rolls. But I still had this party to set up for that night, so I got back to work. When I saw her returning later, I assumed she was going to have another go at me, and I'll admit I was scared. But she never said a word, appearing to have forgotten the whole incident! She led with fear, and that's how she got people to work for her and do whatever she wanted, while paying as little as possible. By the way, Party #1 and Party #2 were both a total success—and no one was ever the wiser as to which guest list they had been put on.

Lesson #1 courtesy of Mrs. B: Stay calm and learn how NOT to engage when you are dealing with someone who is clearly out of touch with reality.

•• ● ● ● ••

Mrs. D and Her Daughter: To say theirs was a strained relationship is a vast understatement, as I was about to find out, and I also had figure out how to manage working with the two of them. I was hired to plan the wedding of Mrs. D's daughter. While I always arrived on time, Mrs. D was not only on time, but waiting for me. Her go-to outfit was a black dress with a white lace collar, black orthopedic shoes, and dark hose. And she always had a scowl on her face. Think Sister Mary Sourpuss from Catholic school.

Our first meeting was at their magnificent home on NYC's Madison Avenue. There, in the living room were two chairs side by side, and one single chair facing them. It looked a bit like either COVID social distancing or a makeshift interrogation room. Mrs. D and her daughter took the two seats side by side, and I sat facing them. No chitchat as Mrs. D started right in telling me everything she wanted and how she expected the wedding to look. She listed off the décor and style she envisioned, the flowers; the tents on the lawn of their waterfront home, north of, New York City; the flow of the wedding; and the music. It was clear Mrs. D had everything all figured out.

I glanced at her daughter, who up to this point hadn't uttered a word. I guessed that the bride-to-be was in her mid-thirties. She looked rather plain. She actually seemed a bit disengaged at first but after her mother's speech? Her face was red and her jaw and fists were clenched. It was just a matter of time before she blew. While I'm very good at sensing the dynamics of the clients I work with, anyone could have read *that* room.

As her mother started in again, finally the daughter lost it—lost it like a two-year-old who's lost her pacifier. She stood up and just launched into Mrs. D, screaming that her mother was NOT going to dictate HER wedding day. Explosive and relentless is the best way to describe her tirade.

And as if the exchange was choreographed, Mrs. D then stood up and started in on her daughter, matching her decibel for decibel. Then her daughter popped up and started in on round two.

And there I sat, in silence, taking it all in. The position of the chairs made it feel even more like I was watching a scene from a movie. The entire time took probably ten minutes but felt like an eternity. I was thinking *How in the hell am I going to manage these two!?* And then, almost as suddenly as it began, they both sat down and turned their attention back to me. Apparently, this type of "communication" was the norm for them.

Once sanity and quiet returned to the room, I said, "If I am going to plan this wedding for you, this is how it's going to work." (BTW, I was making this up on the spot, but I knew I had to get control of the situation immediately.) I turned to Mrs. D. and said, "I will *never* meet with the two of you together again. I will meet with you, and then," I continued, addressing the daughter, "I will meet with you. I will listen to both of your requests then determine how it will play out so the style and design are seamless."

Crickets for a few moments, then they both looked at me and said, "Fine." Honestly, I think they were both relieved knowing they didn't actually need to talk to each other to pull this wedding off.

Logistically, this was an intense production. We needed multiple tents, flooring, and air conditioning units for the tents, in addition to the regular wedding décor. Working with me for two solid weeks before the nuptials were teams of experts as well as rigging trucks and men to help erect the tents. I drove from the city north to check on the final touches on the Friday evening before the Saturday wedding. As I arrived at the D family's beautiful waterfront home, I thought how the tents looked great and was reveling in the fact that we were actually a little bit ahead of schedule.

All of a sudden, I heard a window open on the back side of the house, facing the water. Mrs. D, scowling and wearing her black nun outfit, yelled, "David!! Where in the fuck are you?!"

I decided to gloss over her tone and vulgarities and replied sweetly, "I'm right here! How are you? Excited about tomorrow?"

She leaned further out the window and pointed at one of the tents. "You need to move this fucking tent RIGHT NOW! It's blocking the view of the water from my bedroom."

For a second, I wondered if she actually had a sense of humor, because this had to be a joke. *Nope. She was serious.* I approached the house cautiously, not at all convinced she wouldn't throw something at me if I got within range. "Mrs. D," I began, "it is impossible to move these tents that it has taken two weeks to install."

"I know! I've been up here all summer and watching."

What the actual hell, I thought. *Why didn't she say something weeks or even days ago?*

Mrs. D continued, "I will write you a check for $100,000 for the tent company to make it happen!"

I took a deep breath and had to explain that in this case money was not going to help. Money can't fix your life or find you love and it sure as hell will *not* get a tent deconstructed and reconstructed in the space of twelve hours so you can get your stupid water view back. Mrs. D slammed the window shut, and I didn't see her again until the next day when my team and I arrived to be on site for the wedding.

I had hoped that at least for her daughter's wedding, she'd wear something more mother-of-the-bride and less nun-in-mourning, but no way. Her entire wardrobe was as dark as her personality: black dress, black hose, black shoes, black mood, even on the wedding day. She gave me the full silent treatment except for when she was instructing me on how to change the timeline, the seating, and even the wedding processional. I am confident this was purely an effort to mess with me and screw her daughter as well.

Lesson #2, courtesy of Mrs. D and her daughter: You have to be the one to educate your client on what can and can't be done. And you have to stand up with confidence to some serious crazy at times to establish realistic expectations.

• • ● ● ● • •

Mrs. G: She hailed from a well-known billionaire family from Latin America that also keeps residences in NYC (and probably a half dozen other cosmopolitan cities). I was called by Mrs. G's assistant to be considered as the planner/designer of her daughter's birthday bash, which would be taking place at a Caribbean island. Well, hell yes, I wanted a gig that would put me in a beautiful Caribbean venue, so I was excited to meet with Mrs. G and seal the deal.

I arrived on time to their gorgeous Park Avenue penthouse, a.k.a., mansion in the sky. I truly had no idea homes like this existed. The stunning private elevator opened up to a ballroom—a legit ballroom–straight out of Versailles, gold-gilded everything, murals on the walls and on the ceiling. I didn't know ahead of time who this family was, but when I found out later, I was like, *oh my*!

Three Latino butlers who didn't speak a word of English escorted me to one of three chairs in the middle of the otherwise opulent but empty ballroom. Since I had experienced the three-chair arrangement before, I assumed the other two seats were for Mrs. G and her daughter. Something else I'd also experienced was The Wait. This time I sat there for two full hours, which gave me a lot of time to think about my options. Leave and definitely lose the job or wait and continue to waste my time. That is one thing about the ultra-rich I cannot stand—the belief that no one else's time has any value.

Finally, Paulo, one of the butlers, popped out of a façade door on the far side of the ballroom, startling the hell out of me. He was pushing what looked like a bar cart. *Well, this is nice,* I thought. *At least I'll get some refreshments.* But as he neared, I didn't see crystal carafes or decanters of top-shelf liquor—I saw nail polishes, files and buffers, and finger bowls. It was a freaking manicure caddy! Paulo positioned the cart between the other two chairs. Then a woman emerged from the same door and walked over and took a seat and prepared her tools. The manicurist. Finally, from yet another secret door Mrs. G strode out and went straight to the other chair, barely saying hello, and never apologizing for the incredible tardiness, not to mention rudeness. She did manage to say we would get started *after* her manicure was done. I guess she can't chew gum and walk at the same time either! So, yes, I sat there and watched this overprivileged woman have her nails done. Given the brevity of our actual conversation about the party, she easily could have spoken with me first and then taken all bloody day for her manicure as far as I was concerned. Mrs. G told me what she wanted and hired me on the spot.

As much as I love my work, planning this party gave me no joy at all, especially with such a demanding mother who set an unrealistic budget. But it was, on a Caribbean Island and it was a brilliant party that thrilled the birthday girl. In retrospect, I think I had the gig before I even showed up, which might explain (though not excuse) our intro meeting. I had the lovely Mrs. C from Bel Air to thank for the referral to Mrs. G. These ladies love to talk . . .

Lesson #3, courtesy of Mrs. G: Know what side your bread is buttered on. No matter how entitled and rude a client is, never ever talk about one to another. And keep the compliments coming—it's what they expect, deserved or not.

• • • • • •

Mrs. F: You will see that Mrs. "F" is quite fitting... She was the second wife to a billionaire, and it was her life's mission to do everything to prove she was better than Wife #1. In this case, planning a birthday party for her husband. She had hired me several times before for parties at her home and for her various charity events in NYC.

Working with Mrs. F always came with strings attached and a lot of quid pro quo that usually ended up being very one-sided. "Give me a great deal on my husband's birthday party (or my birthday or my daughters' bat mitzvahs), and I'll make sure to introduce you to [fill in the blank]." And blank is usually what I got with Mrs. F. As a business owner who relies on word of mouth, I always take my chances and sometimes suffer some losses, but I always hope for the best. Working with Mrs. F never did lead to referrals to other clients.

It was time for our menu tasting for her husband's party, and all was going well . . . until the French fries came out, beautifully displayed on each of the place settings. Mrs. F took one bite and practically spit it out. "Unacceptable and uneatable," she said. (I didn't tell her the word was actually "inedible." And by the way, they tasted fine to me!) I mean, this isn't the entrée we are talking about but a *side dish*.

Regardless, this started us on a trek of six, yes, six separate dates to taste French fries. Mrs. F graded the level of salt, the oil used to fry them in, and the "crunch" in the bite. She even took into consideration the relative humidity of where the fries were made, compared with that of the venue where she was throwing the party. I felt truly sorry for the poor catering crew who had to replicate the fries. I am confident she cared more about the quality of the fries than she cared about her husband or her kids! At least the sixth try was a charm, or close enough as the case may be. Mrs. T deemed them acceptable. Not remarkable but acceptable. By this time, I was so freaking over the French fries, I wanted to shove them in her mouth so she couldn't talk.

As the party date approached, Mrs. F was obsessed with the seating assignments. I arranged for a top tier headline entertainer to perform, and, believe me, that was the easiest part of the entire party! Many of her guests were divorced and remarried or with new significant others, so she wanted to make sure no one was sitting near someone that would make them uncomfortable. Seating a dinner like this requires accuracy, not just for organization but for the staff, since the kitchen and waiters need to know which meal goes to which guest.

At 4:30 p.m. on the day of the party, which was to start at 6:30, Mrs. F said to me, "Screw the fucking seating chart" (did I mention her potty mouth?) and preceded to hand me all the name cards. She instructed me to put them in a box and let the guests pull out a card that would indicate where to sit. It was like a sadistic key party. Of course, this was a recipe for disaster, but she walked away to let me and my team deal with the fallout. Some guests actually left because of the possibility that they would be seated near, or worse, at a table with their exes and new partners.

Mrs. F was one of those clients who liked to say I was "part of the family" after I'd done enough events for her. But, in reality, I got treated like the help and never like the professional designer that I was. It's an odd dynamic, and one I've never felt comfortable with, but I knew I'd have to find a way to do so as I moved forward in my industry.

Lesson #4, courtesy of Mrs. French Fry: Bite your tongue and accept there are some people who gain their sense of self-worth by railroading other people to do their bidding. Realize how miserable they are inside and be thankful you're not like them.

•• ● ● ● ••

Mrs. K: Ah, the lovely Mrs. H and her equally lovely husband and adult children, cough cough. Not sure if it was nature or nurture, but this family knew they could get whatever they wanted, however and whenever they wanted. A clan of monsters that thrived on being nasty. I was hired to create their daughter's wedding at their New England estate. The issue: I was given tasks that fell far outside of what I was contracted to do. Such as the demand to devise a hurricane evacuation plan three weeks before the wedding. Had this been in Florida, in hurricane season, I'd have applauded the forethought. In fact, I have indeed created hurricane evacuation plans. But it was in New England and nowhere near hurricane season! It was simply a hoop Mrs. K wanted me to jump through, just for the sake of it. She loved to change directions, change floor plans at the last minute, and never provided a proper seating chart or gave me guest names. It was like a puzzle with pieces missing—impossible. She never smiled (nor did her family); never expressed gratitude. It can be very hard to work for people like this, but you still need to do your very best and give 100 percent no matter who the client is . . . or what they ask for.

Lesson #5, courtesy of Mrs. K and family: Put on your party armor and get ready for battle. You will be the winner if you stand out and do brilliant work. Trust me, someone in the crowd will be watching, and you will be hired.

••••••

Mrs. P: We all know that mothers love to "help" plan their daughters' weddings. But I've seen my share of mothers (always wealthy beyond imagination) who simply take over the planning. Maybe because they are paying for it (or their husbands are), they figure it's their *right* to dictate every detail. Maybe they are living vicariously and planning the wedding they wished *they* had had but couldn't afford at the time. All I know is Mrs. P took this to extremes. She wanted me to turn a lovely venue near their home into the South of France. Okay, aside from the fact that venue looks nothing like the South of France, I assured her I would do my best!

Mrs. P called my office incessantly after she hired me. Non-stop. And she always sounded like she was screaming. Some women have resting bitch face. This woman had resting bitch volume—always. She just always sounded like she was angry and pissed off at everyone, all the time. (As an aside, the *only* time I ever met the father of the bride was when he walked her down the aisle. I'm certain he was terrified of his insane wife and gave her a wide berth unless he had no other choice.)

Earlier I shared how I had to keep Mrs. P and her daughter separate in order to plan the latter's wedding. Well, Mrs. P's daughter threw a whole new wrench into things. She called me one day to confide that she had become pregnant at the beginning of the wedding planning process. I was sworn to secrecy, and under no circumstances whatsoever was I to inform her mother. The issue was: How were we going to alter her wedding gown to disguise her pregnancy? First, let's do a little math. We started planning ten months before the wedding date. She got pregnant three months in and would be seven months pregnant on the big day. So, what in the hell was I supposed to do here? Spandex will not hide a baby bump in the third trimester!

So, the plan we hatched was to keep letting the gown out in small increments, so hopefully her mother would not notice. Ha! I considered designing a huge, cascading bouquet that might hide her bump *if* she never let go of the thing throughout the ceremony and reception, which, of course, was impossible. (God help me, but I was thinking about the huge floral casket drapes I saw so often at my father's funeral home!) Luckily for me, the bride broke down and told her mother the truth, which released me from this charade and allowed me to get on with the business of planning the actual wedding!

A few days later, Mrs. P phoned screaming, as usual, that she had to meet with me ASAP. Shortly thereafter, she came flying into my offices in her PJs! You can't make this shit up! PJs, robe, no makeup, bedhead—it was as if she had literally woken up, called me hysterically from her bed, and then came straight over. Mrs. P then proceeded to curl up into a fetal position in the chair across from my desk and started sobbing and rocking herself. All I could think: she was either off her meds or took too many! Therapist was *not* in my job description. But, in reality, a wedding planner does often assume the role of therapist throughout what can be a very emotional and stressful process. Crazy thing is, she was blubbering so much, to this day I have no idea what she said or what was wrong. Makes me wonder if she really accidentally came to my office instead of her therapist's!

Fast forward to the wedding. The bride, clearly with child, looked radiant and beautiful. Things were going off without a hitch . . . until her ex-fiancé showed up in the middle of the festivities, drunk off his ass, looking as though he wanted to pummel the groom. I donned another "hat"— security guard! I called 911 and kept the jilted ex from interrupting the wedding. The police arrived, hauled him off, and no one among the wedding party or guests ever knew how close things came to a disaster.

Lesson #6, *courtesy of Mrs. P. and company: Accept the fact that wedding planner is but one of the many hats you will wear in this job. Designer, therapist, mediator, confidante, magician . . . bouncer! Whatever it takes to get to the end game of a beautiful wedding.*

•••••••

Mrs. M: I've left the best for last here. I mean, this one tops them all. I always assume I can handle whatever is thrown my way—learn as you go and make it up on the spot much of the time. But this evening, at the epic and stunning Cipriani's on 42nd Street in midtown NYC, I was faced with a scenario where I said to myself, *what do you do when you don't know what to do?* Or to put it bluntly, *this is a shit storm, and I have to figure out immediately what to do!* There was no handbook or previous experience to lean on to teach me how to handle what was about to come my way.

To better set up this insane night, I have to go back two years earlier when Mrs. M called me to plan and design her oldest daughter's wedding. For future reference, she had two daughters. I had worked in the past for Mrs. M, and she was elegant, direct, always knew what she wanted, and made it clear when she there was something she didn't like. Mrs. M never minced words and didn't belabor the point. She just said what she had to say and moved on. I actually appreciated this because it meant there were no gray areas for me to figure out and hope for the best.

Mrs. M's daughter was excited to have her wedding planned and designed by me. Contracts were signed, deposits were made, and meetings began. I secured Cipriani's, which is one of my favorite venues in NYC. This venue is *always* booked and hardly ever available on a Saturday night, so I was beyond thrilled to come back and share this news with Mrs. M and her daughter—that this impossible-to-book venue was locked down and paid for.

I scheduled the first meeting with Mrs. M and her oldest daughter to begin the journey of figuring out the look, the style, the colors, the menu, and all of the typical details I need to plan any event. We were moving along quite nicely . . . until radio silence. I stopped hearing from either Mrs. M or the bride. I made calls, sent emails, and continued to reach out but no reply. Silence is deadly in my profession. I need insight, details, direction, and approvals, otherwise I am literally left in the dark.

What do you do when you don't know what to do? What do you do when your client ghosts you? Weeks and weeks passed with no communication. Then I received a call from Mrs. M. In her typical fashion, the call was short, direct, and curt. Not to mention stomach-dropping awful.

"David, I have to share some news. The wedding has been canceled."

Dumbfounded, I asked if it was being postponed or delayed or simply canceled?

Mrs. M said, "It's OFF. It's not happening. Keep the deposit for a future party; call the vendors." And she hung up.

Of course, I was curious to know what in God's name had happened. This was no small wedding. The venue is one of the most expensive in the city, and the vendors I had contracted were all top-notch and pricey experts whom I knew would please the parents and the bride. But Mrs. M gave me my marching orders and I was off, sadly, to make all my calls. It took just about two days to inform all the vendors. Party Planned. Party Designed. Party Canceled. Just like that. Life goes on, new clients come in, business goes on. It's the circle of life for a wedding planner.

A year later, my assistant came into my office and said Mrs. M wants to talk with you immediately. I am thinking Mrs. M as in short-and-to-the-point Mrs. M? *Yep, she is back!*

I always noticed her calls never began or ended with a hello, goodbye, or thank you. She just started right in. "David, my younger daughter is engaged, and I want to use the deposits from my oldest daughter's wedding and apply it to my younger daughter's. I would like to come in with her as soon as possible to start the planning and designing." And she hung up.

Some things never change. A meeting was scheduled, and we planned the details swiftly and easily with the bride and the groom. Everything regarding this wedding and my work was going perfectly . . . that is, until the day of the wedding. Here is where the shit really hit the fan . . .

The flowers were stunning, the tables set to the nines. Fantastic tablecloths, elegant place settings, a thirty-piece orchestra, and a *chuppah* to die for. It was a Jewish ceremony at its finest. The chuppah was covered with flowers and had fabric drapery (remember this), and the room was illuminated with magnificent lighting. There was a custom dance floor and massive floral creations in urns on pedestals throughout the entire venue. It was truly breathtaking!

We were now two hours out before show time, or when the actual ceremony processional would begin. At this point, we were lining up the wedding party to run a rehearsal so everyone would understand the flow and order of the procession and where to stand during the ceremony. Basic stuff. Typically, it takes a little time to get settled down because everyone is excited, the wedding party is talking, and no one is listening to me and my staff. Finally, we got ready to start, and then Mrs. M asked, "Where is my daughter?" (referring to her eldest daughter, the one whose wedding was supposed to take place in this same venue a year earlier).

I paused the rehearsal to look for the bride's sister, which didn't take long. I just had to follow the sound of her wailing to the far back of the venue. Her cries were echoing throughout the cavernous space. She was out of her bloody gourd. This daughter was also the Maid of Honor for her sister's big day. There are responsibilities that come with this title: making sure to take care of the bride, in this case her sister; bustling the bride's wedding gown; making sure she looks just perfect; representing the family under the *chuppah;* and so on. Plus, she was to deliver a beautiful, loving Maid of Honor speech at the celebration. How in the hell was this banshee going to manage all that?

Once I got the elder Miss M to stop screaming, I had to figure out what in the world was wrong with her. Gulping air and mascara streaming down her face, she was insistent and inconsolable that this was HER day, not her sister's. SHE was supposed to be married first, "not my stupid little sister!" So, basically she was having a giant tantrum over what she wanted and couldn't have. Anyone with young children will understand this—but this was a grown woman.

I slowly brought her into the processional line to explain to her what we were doing. It was right at this moment that I realized I had an even bigger issue: the Maid of Honor was drunk or on something (or things), and she was completely out of it. *What do I do?* I had no choice but to continue with the rehearsal, knowing I had about ninety minutes or so to get her sober before the wedding began.

Everyone was watching the Maid of Honor during the rehearsal. She could barely stand up, let alone walk down the aisle toward the *chuppah*. Somehow, we made it through the rehearsal, and I pulled aside the Maid of Honor to have a little chat again. I told her that she really had to pull it together for her sister and her family to save herself from looking childish and foolish to all the guests that were going to be at the wedding. She glared at me and stormed away like a seven-year-old that couldn't get her way, which was true . . . she couldn't have her wedding first!

Fast forward to "go time," as in the guests had arrived and the orchestra was playing, the rabbi was waiting, and the full bridal party was lined up for the processional to begin. There were music cues for each of the various key attendants before they would walk down the aisle. Honestly, it was like a mini-Jewish Broadway show.

I looked over to the full wedding party to see if we could start on time, if everyone was ready, and I noticed that our Maid of Honor was FAR WORSE than before. *Wasn't anyone except me noticing her condition?* Why didn't someone babysit her for a bit, for she was totally acting like a baby! She couldn't stand up straight and was swaying in place. She had tossed her hair into a rat's nest, and her makeup was completely running down her face.

What do you do when you really, really don't know what to do? I turned around and headed straight for Mrs. M and Mr. M (who had never uttered a word to me throughout the planning of either of his daughters' weddings). They had their arms linked and were ready to receive the bride to escort her down the aisle. I asked them to please speak to their eldest daughter and get her childish behavior under control. I thought this was reasonable, to enlist the parents to take care of the situation. Surely, they'd had some practice over the years, right?

Mrs. M looked straight into my eyes and said, "YOU deal with her. We will not!"

To say I was shocked—and a bit panicked—is an understatement.

I decided the best course was to have the Maid of Honor sit this one out—to *not* participate in the wedding processional, as crazy as that seemed. I asked her to go somewhere quiet to gather herself and join the party after the ceremony. Well, you can imagine how well *that* went over. I didn't have time for this shit; I had to turn back to the task at hand—the freaking wedding was about to start!

It was show time. Music was cued, and the orchestra segued into the official music for the ceremony. Everyone in the wedding party was holding their breath as I was trying to handle a potential nightmare. It's not that people didn't notice the brewing storm. It's just that no one tried to do anything to help me stop it!

Step by step, the wedding party gracefully and elegantly glided down the aisle toward the rabbi under the *chuppah*. It was now time for me to cue the Maid of Honor despite every fiber in my being knowing that this was wrong. (*She* knew it was the wrong thing to do, her parents didn't give a damn, and they put it all on me. Incredulously, even the bride, who clearly knew what was happening, didn't seem to care either!) What was freaking wrong with these people? Oh right . . . they were delusional and selfish!

In one final, last-ditch effort, I grabbed the Maid of Honor's shoulders and shook her and raised my voice, saying, "Look at me! No, look me right in the eyes and listen to me! If you do this, you will make a total fool out of yourself."

"But I have to," she slurred. "I have a speech to give."

"Honey, you can't even put two words together. Here," I said, handing her my notes. "Try and read this here."

Of course, she couldn't! And by the way, the parents were watching me this whole time and doing NOTHING, literally NOTHING. I looked at them, imploring them one last time to step up and step in. Nothing doing. Mrs. M held her hand up like a traffic cop, as if to say *stop* and *move* this along. So, I did just that: I sent the angry, selfish, drunk, stoned brat down the aisle.

She looked like a drunken pirate on a rolling ship, swaying from one side of the aisle to the other. What must have been two minutes felt like two hours—two horrible, cringe-inducing hours. The elder Miss M made it to the steps of the *chuppah* platform, where she needed to take three steps up to get to her assigned place. I held my breath and simply just hoped she had it in her. *What else could I do?* First step, second step, and then third step . . . she made it!

But then she got disoriented and wandered to the back side of the stage, losing her balance and grabbing the beautifully installed and designed drapery along the entire back of the room that created a lovely backdrop. This is where it went from bad to really, really bad. Time slowed down, I swear. I watched from the back of the venue as she grasped the drapes and fell backward off the stage. It was like she vanished and was never there.

When she had refused to bow out, I knew something bad was going to happen. So, I had planned for the absolute worst case scenario. I positioned two of my coordinators behind the drapes just in case the Maid of Honor passed out or fell or both. That way my team could snatch her, give her smelling salts, and take her away. After the ceremony, I approached two of her friends, and I demanded that they remove her from the venue—making her disappear for good this time.

The next morning, my office phone rang and it was Mrs. M. "David! It was such a lovely wedding! So stunning and elegant and grand! It was a great night! And one more thing. Thank you for what you did."

I sat stunned for a minute. *Holy shit. Mrs. M said thank you??*

Lesson #7, courtesy of Mrs. M and her immature, narcissistic elder daughter: What do you do when you don't know what to do? Expect the worst and put a plan in place.

CHAPTER 12

How My Fair Wedding Saved My Life

So often the things that change our lives aren't the ones we planned for. Despite probably being best known for my TV shows, I never looked for a career in TV. Call it luck or good timing, but looking back, I see it as fate stepping in. I had no idea what I was getting into when TV found me, but to say it changed my life is an understatement.

My dreams of acting professionally got squashed early on, but that allowed me to focus my energy and creativity on growing my event- and wedding-planning business. I was able to work with some pretty remarkable people in some of the world's most beautiful places. In one year alone, I ended up getting the job to plan the official post-Grammys party—for 4,000 guests! I also planned the Kennedy Center Gala for the first time that year, and I invited my parents so they could meet Andrea Bocelli, who was making his U.S. debut. Suffice to say that between star-studded events like these and my ongoing work designing weddings and parties around the world, I was a pretty happy camper.

When I was first invited to be on *The View*, as word of my party planning work was getting around, I was an absolute nervous wreck, and I was certain it showed. So when they invited me back, I was shocked. And they kept inviting me back until eventually I was offered a standing gig with Barbara Walters and the others, which turned into a fantastic, fun five-year run as *The View's* entertaining expert.

During my time on the show, I avoided the Green Room at all costs. I sat in there one or two times and it wasn't for me. It's where all the A-list guests would hang out until they were called to the set. But the thought of being in that space literally terrified me. I didn't—and still don't—see myself as a celebrity, and I felt completely out of place there. I was just a guy trying to elevate his career and inspire others in planning their celebrations. In order for me to have my five minutes of fame on *The View*, I opted to wait in my little dressing room until it was time for me to go on.

What was really fun, however, was walking down the hallway to see which celebrities would be on the show the same day as me. Among the names on the dressing-room doors were Uma Thurman, George Clooney, Mariah Carey, Hugh Jackman, Eva Longoria, and Mary J. Blige, among others. I was as star-struck as anyone!

Something I didn't know during those five years is that creator and executive producer Bill Geddie was watching me closely, and was, in fact, grooming me for something even bigger. One day after filming *The View*, Bill invited me into his office at ABC. He sat me down and said, "You are ready to have your own show."

I'm sure my jaw dropped to the floor. He went on to explain we needed to build a longer fifteen-minute segment on *The View* that I would showcase your work.

If that was well received (it was, whew!), then we would create a pilot to shop around to the networks. Bill asked one of *The View* cohosts, Star Jones, to throw a party at her home in The Hamptons that I would plan for the pilot of *The Party Planner*.

Was I excited? Absolutely. I was also overwhelmed and underprepared. To this point, I'd only done my short segments on *The View*. But I was ready to bring this to life, and I was at once eager and scared. Bill was a consummate professional and an incredible mentor. He coached me on how to be at ease in front of the camera as well as how to treat the cast and crew with respect.

Another big difference for me with *The Party Planner* was that the show would include an in-depth interview with the party host, in this case Star Jones for the pilot. This aspect was completely new to me.

The day before I was to interview Star, Bill took me aside. "I'm going to teach you everything I taught Barbara Walters for her sit-down interviews."

And thank God he did; I was being trained by the very best. He taught me how to listen, how to engage, and how to take a beat and pause to let the guest respond, which is usually when you get the best stuff. And, if I say so myself, I knocked it out of the park with Star (thank you, Bill!). The filming of the party itself, packed with Star's friends and celebrity buddies, went off perfectly. Only thing left was to edit it into the pilot and send it out to the networks. Once that was done, Bill and I pitched the show to the Discovery Channel, who loved the concept. We left the meeting feeling very positive.

I hit the road to create some buzz, appearing on talk shows hosted by Tony Danza, Wendy Williams, Ricki Lake, Queen Latifah, Bonnie Hunt, and Wayne Brady, among others. It was a blast. And I was on my way back to the hotel after appearing on Wayne's show when Bill called with some news: the network we were hoping would greenlight thirteen episodes decided to only go for four specials. I was disappointed, but not for long.

The next morning Bill called back. "Are you sitting down?" he asked. *Jesus,* I thought, *did they decide to take a pass on the four specials?* Nope, and it was thing good thing Bill had me sit down before he delivered the news.

"In addition to the four specials, they want sixty-five episodes! Are you ready because you are about to enter TV boot camp!"

Such is the mercurial, crazy world of television. You can feel crushed one moment and overjoyed the next. "I'm ready!" I nearly shouted into the phone.

And so my career in TV began in earnest. *The Party Planner* was an amazing, exhausting, exhilarating experience. That said, I was devastated to find out it wasn't picked up again after its initial run. Oh, well, it was fun while it lasted.

I will admit that after all the work, time, heart, and soul I put into that show, I was bruised and felt adamant about leaving the world of TV behind. My business had definitely grown more with all of the exposure from *The Party Planner*, so I tried to look at that bright side. But while I had decided I was done with TV, TV wasn't done with me. A network rep repeatedly called my offices in NYC, asking my publicist if I would be interested in a show they wanted me to do. I said, "No, absolutely not." But I guess taking no for an answer isn't how these folks get things done. After rebuffing them four times, I finally asked my publicist to find out where they were located, and it turns out they were mere blocks from my office. *Huh. Was that the universe talking?* I figured it didn't cost me much to walk over and see what they had in mind.

I met with Kim Martin, the brand new president of the WETV network, and she pitched the concept for *My Fair Wedding*. While I wanted to be aloof and blasé about the whole thing (that was my bruised ego talking), I just couldn't be. I fell in love, love, love with the idea right then and there. It was the first show Kim greenlighted in her new role. And it was the start of a journey that could not have come at a more perfect time for me. I was in the middle of an abusive, codependent relationship that was killing me on the inside. What people saw outwardly was an enthusiastic, energetic, happy man who loved his job planning parties and helping people create wonderful celebrations. And all of that was true—but none of that joy had reflected back into my heart, to my personal story.

Once I said yes to the offer, I threw everything I had into *My Fair Wedding*. The initial concept was to take couples' misguided ideas or wedding themes that needed a bit of help. I was to listen to what they *really* wanted and make it come true. I took my role very seriously and considered it an honor to be invited into the lives of so many couples during one of the most important times of their relationship. There were couples facing challenges, overcoming hardships or tragedies, and I made it my mission to lift them up and send them down the aisle with delight, grace, and happiness.

After long days of filming the show I would call my executive producer Lasta and tell her I felt there was so much more going on here than just over-the-top weddings. The feedback I received from viewers echoed my feelings—everyone was getting so much pleasure from watching other people experience joy! I realized you really *do* get back what you put into the world. The joy was reciprocal and being in the very heart of these circles was healing *me* as well. When I saw the love, trust, and mutual respect these couples had for one another, I knew those things were possible for me, too. I think the success of the show is what really brought the terrible dysfunction of my personal life into focus. I started seeing a very good therapist to help me navigate my relationship and work on my codependency issues. So when I say *My Fair Wedding* saved my life, I am not exaggerating. The couples I worked with were my lifeline to happiness and a distraction from my own life, which was a mess at that time.

It's impossible to choose any favorite couples from the show because every single one of them gave me something special and lasting. But I want to share a few of the stories with you that are especially close to my heart.

The Dragonfly Bride: Everyone knows any bride is beautiful. But I had one bride who just couldn't see herself that way. Regina didn't have that bride-to-be glow, was quite shy, soft-spoken, and seemed burdened. It didn't take me long to see what the problem was once I caught the dynamic between Regina and her mother. You see, her mother was stunning and outgoing, showing up at our meetings with impeccable hair, makeup, and clothes. She made a point of telling Regina her hair was a mess or criticized what she was wearing. Clearly, in her mother's mind, *she* was the star, and her daughter was merely a backup. Regina, quite clearly, had never been made to feel beautiful. Quite the opposite. All I could think of was Snow White's narcissistic stepmother looking into her magic mirror!

Regina wanted a wedding full of dragonflies and fairies. No problem there, but I saw what I also needed to do was build her confidence and help her see herself as beautiful. I'll admit it took a lot of patience, but I worked with her those three weeks of filming. I had her look into a real mirror and say, "I AM beautiful!" On the day of the wedding, as I stood with her before she walked down the aisle, I asked, "How do you feel?"

She said she was excited and happy. But I saw more—Regina was an absolutely beautiful bride, who stood tall and confident.

I asked, "But do you feel beautiful?"

She began to cry and said in a strong voice, "Yes! I am beautiful!"

•• • ● ● • ••

A Make-A-Wish Dream Comes True: The Make-A-Wish Foundation is such an incredible organization, granting wishes to children with critical illnesses—be it a trip to Disneyland or meeting a favorite person like a baseball player or musician. But the selfless, loving wish of Ryan, a seventeen-year-old recovering from a bout with cancer, humbled and floored me: He wanted me to plan a beautiful wedding for his mother, Wendy. Because she worked so hard at caring for him during his illness, she didn't have the time or money to plan the wedding she dreamed of with her fiancé, Rocco. I focused this episode around their small, close-knit town in Kansas, enlisting the help of their friends, local shop owners, and her church to plan a gorgeous wedding for Wendy and Rocco, making the bride feel like the princess she deserved to be. Let me tell you, there was not a dry eye in that town on that day, including the crew and me!

•• • ● ● • ••

A Real-Life Disney Princess: Aurora just wanted to be a princess for her wedding. And I remember thinking how fitting, since she shared the same name as Sleeping Beauty. She lived a simple life but had a big dream for her wedding, which unfortunately she didn't have the resources to fulfill. When we first met, I found a shy, quiet young woman who lacked confidence. As soon as I heard her story, I called my friends at Disney and planned a soup-to-nuts wedding for her at Walt Disney World, starting with getting dressed in Cinderella's castle. Her attendants were the other Disney princesses, and she and her Prince Charming rode in a horse-drawn Cinderella coach to her ceremony. Aurora became a real-life Disney princess that day, exhibiting grace and elegance at almost every moment. Well, there was that one moment where she fell to her knees, crying in happiness and disbelief. Can you say Happily Ever After?

• • ● ● ● • •

A Hawai'ian Wedding in Southern California: While typically it was the bride who reached out to *My Fair Wedding*, in one case we got a call from a groom who wanted to make sure his bride would be happy on their wedding day. Kristin had recently suffered a stroke at a very young age, and was understandably down. The groom wanted so badly to make sure her wedding day was incredibly special, filled with much-needed happiness, love, and fun. He came to us because he just didn't know how to make it happen. Together we landed on a Hawai'ian-themed wedding and decided to really do it up. We wanted to make sure the life she was now living was worth celebrating. Hawai'ian colors, flowers, food, and décor were capped off with a brilliant fireworks show that surprised everyone. When the bride came running into my arms, sobbing and smiling, I knew that we gave her the joy her groom had wanted.

• • ● ● ● • •

Kids Do the Darnedest Things: We hear a lot of stories about how self-involved and indifferent kids are these days. But this one group of school children from Palm Springs, California, certainly gave me hope for the future. Their teacher, Kim, was recovering from breast cancer and had lost much of her hair from the treatment. Her class wanted her to have a super-special wedding day and asked *My Fair Wedding* what we could do. I designed an all-pink extravaganza to support breast cancer awareness and surprised Kim with an appointment with a stylist who fitted her with a stunning wig. She literally floated down the aisle that day, with her students among the happy guests.

•• • ● ● ● ••

Romeo and Juliet with a Happier Ending: One show that touched me deeply was the wedding of a Jewish bride Shirley and a Chinese Christian groom Andy. This was a sweet, kind, and loving couple who were carrying a large boulder of pain with them to their nuptials. Her parents were against the wedding from the very start. Perhaps because of the rift with my own father, I truly empathized with the bride's sadness that her parents could not accept her groom because he was not Jewish. All through the planning, I tried to convince the bride's parents how badly their daughter wanted them there on her special day. Right before the wedding started, the bride's mother arrived. It turns out she drove herself to be there for her daughter. We were all so excited . . . until the bride's father also arrived, having followed his wife in his own car, and demanded that she leave at once.

I asked the heartbroken bride who would be walking her down the aisle, and she replied, "No one."

I promised her that would NOT happen and asked if she would grant me the privilege of walking with her down the aisle. I know all too well the pain of one's parents not accepting you for your choices and was honored to be by her side. She was beyond grateful, and I know it made the world of difference to her in that moment.

•• • ● ● ● ••

Something that I've never divulged before is that I made it a condition with my crew to never film me crying. Trust me, I cried during every single episode of *My Fair Wedding*. But I never, ever wanted to shift the attention onto me. My job was to bring dream weddings to life and to bring joy to the couples and the viewers, who I knew had become so engaged in the stories of our many couples. I got dubbed The Fairy Godfather, which was fine by me. I came, sprinkled some fairy dust, then disappeared!

My Fair Wedding, which morphed into *David Tutera Unveiled*, and then *David Tutera Celebrations* ran for ten years. Think about it, it was a decade of MY LIFE, and it was one of the most exhausting yet rewarding times of my life. Giving those couples a beautiful start to their new lives together, and knowing our audience vicariously went on the journeys with us, was incredible. There was as much laughter as there were tears. Audiences loved waiting to see which dress I selected out of the three the bride tried on. In fact, that was one of my favorite parts of the show—surprising the bride on her wedding day with the dress that fit her perfectly. Everything about *My Fair Wedding* was magical, including the way our producer, editors, and crew naturally brought the love, joy, and beauty of every wedding to the screen.

Some might be surprised to know I never once watched any episodes after they were edited and aired. I wanted to remain "me" in the moment when we were shooting. I felt like watching myself after the fact might make me self-conscious and perhaps change the spontaneity of the show. I always wanted it to be about the bride, the families, and the viewers.

Fast forward. My oldest daughter Cielo recently came across *My Fair Wedding* on a streaming platform and got so excited. She could not wait to sit next to me and watch an episode together. After the first one, she turned to me and said, "Daddy, I love you for caring so much for this bride and her family. I am so proud of you!"

As we continued to sit and watch other episodes, my three-year-old Gracie joined us, loving seeing Daddy on TV! Cielo would ask questions about the bride's dress, the bridesmaids' dresses, and all the decisions I made for my wedding couples. She wanted to know specifically why I made certain choices. And I was astonished at how closely Gracie followed right along. She always asked about the cake and the flowers, and couldn't wait to see what happened at the end of each show. Inevitably, whatever was happening on screen, I was there on the couch with both girls nestled right up against me. Once I looked at Cielo to see what she was thinking, and she just gave me the biggest hug. Let me just say it doesn't get any better.

Watching each show for the first time with my two girls will always be the icing on the wedding cake for me. The joy and happiness I feel inside is overwhelming!

I would like to believe that maybe it was all meant to happen in this order . . . to create the show that my girls would eventually watch and come to realize that everyone deserves to be happy and to find joy! The show still airs around the globe, and I humbly suggest if you are looking for an hour of hope and positivity, try to catch an episode.

Lives were changed during *My Fair Wedding*, not least of which was mine. This is the first time I have revealed how much doing this show helped me. So, when I say I am grateful for the opportunity, I mean it from the depths of my heart. I'm truly not sure what would have become of me if not for *My Fair Wedding*. It gave me a reason to get up in the morning and turn my focus on the couples, the crew, and the fans I adored—and still do. I love it when someone approaches me to tell me how much they loved the show and asks if I will ever do it again. Believe me, I would in a heartbeat. I have been so lucky to be a conduit for bringing people happiness, and was extremely fortunate to do that in a venue that reached millions.

My Fair Wedding exploded my business and brought me to a whole new world. I started my first wedding dress and jewelry lines, authored books, and became a household name. I appeared on other TV shows, on soap operas, in commercials (again finally? After how many years?), and the DT brand has been seen and mentioned in movies.

What's funny is how many people ask me to reveal my "favorite" celeb-rities. I pause for a moment or two and, of course, have to refrain from answering. But I will say I've had the honor of working with some truly wonderful people, including Elton John, Prince Charles, Nancy Reagan, Vanessa Williams, and countless ambassadors and presidents from around the globe.

I still have to remind myself of where I started . . . a far cry from singing telegrams in a chicken suit, that's for sure! I am so grateful that I finally took that fourth phone call and headed five blocks south on that day to meet the president of a network who offered me an opportunity that changed my life. You see, you never know what lies ahead of you. So when opportu-nities arise, take that chance. What is the worst that can happen? It might actually turn out to be the best thing that ever happened to you. It could change your life!

CHAPTER 13

My Guy

As someone who has helped countless couples celebrate finding true love and sharing their lives together, you'd think I'd have been better at finding it myself. Trust me, I tried. For most of my life I was looking for love in all the wrong places, or, more accurately, in all the wrong faces. Anyone who knows me knows I truly believe that the joy is in the journey, but damn! I had no idea how long that journey would be, and it often felt like I was on a trek over mountains with no map, no compass, and no idea when I'd reach my destination. So I guess this was the universe telling me to walk the talk—enjoy the journey.

I was dating. And I did enjoy the dates (some of them), laughed when a date was a total disaster, and I felt the thrill of excitement when there was the possibility that THIS one might be THE one. Plus, working with so many amazing couples on *My Fair Wedding* definitely bolstered my belief that one day I would find MY GUY. Being loved and accepted for who I am was really all I wanted. I didn't think I was asking too much.

Just for kicks, let me tell you a bit about some of the men I dated over the course of time:

There was the brain surgeon—brilliant to the point of being too smart. I think because he was so intelligent and skilled, he was bored with anyone who couldn't keep up, which, in turn, made him boring.

How about the hairdressers? (Yes, I dated more than one.) Too bad the ones I dated could never focus and were all over the place, literally and figuratively. But they always had great hair!

Getting my vote for one of the worst encounters was the politician I dated for a while. He was a hyper-overachiever who never had time for me. And his need to always be seen and "on" may have been necessary for his career, but it was death to building a relationship.

Tanning salon receptionist? Let's just say I wish I'd just gone to Florida for the weekend and sat in the sun instead of walking through *that* door.

Remember Michael, the dog groomer? I chalk that one up to young love, first love. My heart was broken, but it was with him that I uncovered my issues of codependency, which took years to work through.

I dated a choreographer once. You'd think with my background and love of musical theater, this would have been a great match. When he wasn't working, he was partying, and as someone who did quite a lot of partying in the past, his lifestyle was too much for me. Plus, like the politician, he needed to stand out in a crowd, always. I didn't.

The fashion designer and I had a lot of fun, but he was so full of himself that there was no room left for anyone else. He went through men like water and, of course, knew *they* were the problem, because he was perfect!

Until looking back and writing this book, I didn't really think about how many medical professionals I have dated. Besides the brain surgeon, there was the eye doctor (whose vision of love was being with someone successful) and the pediatrician. (Lovely, sweet man, but he was always too exhausted from work to ever want to do anything. Nap time was his favorite time.)

Male models. The stereotype is true, at least the ones I went out with: gorgeous airheads. The actors I dated had more depth, but they were always dealing with rejection (I remember how I felt when I didn't get a callback), and that made them incredibly needy.

And then there was the lawyer. The married lawyer. He somehow failed to mention his wife and two-year-old daughter to me before I said yes to a date. Clearly, he was dealing with some major fundamental issues (his sexuality, fidelity, honesty, just to name a few). I bolted the minute I found out the truth.

But there were relationships in my life that shook me to my core: Michael was one of them. As an addict, he challenged me spiritually, emotionally, physically, and psychologically. The longer I stayed trying to help/fix/change him (thanks, codependency!), the harder it was for me to see how he was dimming my light and sapping any peace of mind I had managed find in my life. My friends begged me to leave, but I loved him and knew he was sick. I ran through my laundry list of "what ifs." *What if I tried harder to show how much I loved him? What if I tried to be more patient and forgiving? What if I was unlovable, because if he loved me he'd work on his addictions?* (Do you see a pattern? All the "what ifs" were about ME—me believing in the delusion that anything I did, good or bad, could have an impact on him and his addictions.)

It's a tragic truth that addicts seem supernaturally drawn to those of us with codependency issues. It's as if they inherently know that once we fall for them, it can be nearly impossible for us to leave. And that is the perfect relationship for an addict: Do whatever I want ("Oh, I could stop if I really wanted to . . ."), treat my partner like shit and then some but be secure in the knowledge that he won't leave because he was conditioned not to. All of the baggage I brought into my relationship with Michael was cemented into full-blown codependency by the time it was over: the anxiety, the fear of abandonment, the shame, and the hope. Yes, hope. It is like a secret code word for codependents because it's the thing we hold onto when everything else is crashing around us. We hope it will get better, but it almost always gets worse.

ıg abuse and the violence and irresponsibility it led to finally
ıe enough to leave. Honestly, it was his sex addiction and dis-
his own safety (let alone mine) that pushed me out. I was abso-
luteıy ified of contracting HIV. Had it only been the drugs, there's a
good chance I would have stayed, sad as that is, because even as far gone as
he was, there was still hope (there's that word again) that he would love me
enough to seek help for his addiction. — *I used to say " hope will kill you*'

Later, I met a man named Eliot, and our relationship was similar to the one
I had shared with Michael. He was younger than me and seemed so kind.
He immediately captured my heart. But it didn't take long for his demons
to emerge–drinking nonstop from morning to night and adding pills to
the mix until he passed out. I had never seen anyone care so little for themselves . . . so, of course, I was the perfect boyfriend! Bring on the caretaking,
enabling, and the other codependent behavior!

I would come to his apartment to find him blacked out and having wet
himself, either lying on the floor or worse, in the bed. On a booze run once,
he totaled his car and proceeded to tell me someone else did it. This wasn't
my first rodeo with this shit, but still I stayed with him. Then there was the
time I found blood-soaked sheets, blood in the hallway, and even blood on
the sidewalk outside the apartment. To this day I have no idea what happened. I did manage to get him into rehab, only to have him check himself
out a few days later. That's what a lot of people don't know—you can't make
them stay. Eliot walked out shortly thereafter, drunk and high, and never
returned.

I really fooled myself into believing I was the one who could reach these
men—that a life of love and happiness with me was so much better than
their addictions. In the beginning, I did see love and kindness in their eyes.
But in time, it was overshadowed by the pain and suffering of their dark
journeys. Everyone knows (even though it doesn't always stop us from trying) that you can't change or fix or even help another person who doesn't
want it for themselves. But what happened was I started to destroy myself.
I became hollow, empty, and depleted. I had to save myself before it was

too late. I had to let go and just get in that lifeboat alone and paddle like hell for the shore.

Both of these relationships taught me, finally, the hard lesson that I needed to learn—to take care of myself, and only myself, for a while. I was gutted, depressed, tired, and lost. I needed to heal, that much I knew. And a lot of therapy showed me how to protect my heart. It took years to mend my soul. These days there is far more awareness and many more resources for understanding and healing from codependency. But back then, being alone just seemed safer, and I started to resign myself to the fact that I was never going to find MY GUY—that life partner who would be there for me, as much as I was for him.

There's a scene in the movie *On Golden Pond* between Katharine Hepburn and Henry Fonda that made me realize the kind of love I was looking for—a love where you look forward to walking the journey of life together. Fonda's character has the beginnings of dementia and gets lost trying to find a place he'd been to a thousand times before. He finds his way back to his wife, frustrated and scared. She realizes just how scared he is, then puts her arms around him, and says, "You're safe you old poop. . . . Listen to me, mister. You're my knight in shining armor. Don't you forget it. You're gonna get back up on that horse, and I'm gonna be right behind you, holding on tight, and away we'll go, go, go." That scene personified what I wanted for myself—a bond, mutual support, and someone with whom I'd always feel safe.

How does the expression go? You find what you're looking for when you stop looking? I spent so many years searching for MY GUY and instead mostly found heartache, disappointment, and pain. I was looking for the "perfect" person, which, of course, doesn't exist. That's like searching for a needle on the ocean floor. So, I quit looking, which wasn't hard as I had a pretty full plate: my TV show took up most of my waking hours and I was awaiting the birth of my daughter through a surrogate. Did I say full plate? I had no idea that it would soon be overflowing!

I got a call one day from a dear friend of mine in Arizona. As soon as she said, "I have a friend with a brother named Joey who is so sweet and nice and handsome . . ." I stopped her cold.

"Hell, *no*," I said. "Not interested, not going to happen." I still needed to breathe and continue to heal. I loved the fact she was thinking of me, but I knew I wasn't ready yet, and I didn't know if I'd ever be. Plus, who in their right mind would want to get involved with a man about to have a baby? *And* I lived in California *and* I was working intensely on my show. Too many obstacles, too soon, too impossible.

My friend listened graciously to my litany of excuses, and, regardless, she made me take down this guy's number. "Just call him someday and see how it goes," she said. "It's just a phone call, not the rest of your life." Funny how life works.

Time passed and I found myself on a rare day off from shooting my TV show, driving down Wilshire Boulevard and thinking, *what could it hurt just to give this guy a call? Just someone new to chat with.* I'll admit I tried to find out a bit about him beforehand. I'm usually pretty good uncovering photos and profiles online, but I couldn't turn up anything on this guy. He clearly had me at a disadvantage because by this time I was extremely Googleable! I figured we'd have a quick, awkward call, but we ended up talking for forty-five minutes. And something remarkable—we found out we'd both been left by our significant others on exactly the same day. Fate? Certainly some interesting synchronicity, at the very least.

For the next seven weeks, Joey and I talked and got to know each other over the phone. Old school dating! I loved it because it kept it simple for both of us and made it harder to rebound into a relationship. I was headed to Australia to produce a multiday event for a big celebrity and told Joey that between the time difference and how busy I would be, we likely wouldn't be able to talk while I was there. But a funny thing happened. As soon as I got to my hotel, I realized how much I really did want talk with him, that I would miss our conversations. He was surprised but pleased to hear from me. I had never, ever just gotten to know someone like this before. Every other man I'd dated I'd met in person and sparks flew, mutual attraction fanned the fires, and next thing I knew I was in a relationship with someone I actually barely knew! Never again.

On my flight to Sydney, I thought maybe it was time that Joey and I should meet. During one of our long-distance calls I asked Joey if he'd like to come to L.A. for a weekend soon. Something else was different for me, and I knew it was a good thing: I finally had healthy boundaries.

"You can either stay in a hotel or in the guest room at my house," I said, establishing some perimeters to honor those hard-earned boundaries. He wholeheartedly agreed.

When Joey arrived at LAX, I was waiting at the bottom of the escalator for him. Sporting a pink shirt with black piping and wearing jeans, he smiled all the way down to meet me. So handsome. Yes, my heart did skip a little beat. Partly from nerves and partly because I'm an event planner professionally, I organized a fun-filled weekend. We had dinner that night, spent the day at Disneyland on Saturday (we both love Disney), and capped off the weekend with a dinner at a fabulous West Hollywood restaurant. Our conversations were as easy and comfortable as they'd been on the phone. Joey was only supposed to stay two days, but he missed his flight because we got caught up in conversation and lost track of time!

It felt great, wonderful in fact. I told him about the baby I was expecting, and he was so excited for me. Everything about him comes from a place of positivity and kindness. He told me about being a yoga instructor and about his time working in the world of finance and for a large retailer. That entire weekend I kept asking myself, *Is this MY GUY?* I wouldn't allow myself to believe it—this total stranger who just fell into my life.

Joey headed back to Arizona that evening, and we continued our long phone calls, going a little deeper, learning more about each other and our pasts. I told him about the anxiety I've lived with my whole life, which was a big risk for me. He was completely understanding about it. We decided to meet again, this time in San Francisco. Joey wanted to take me to the Walt Disney Family Museum there. And we took long walks, had great dinners, and even biked across the Golden Gate Bridge. And in the evening, he played meditation music and held me to help alleviate my anxiety. No one had ever been so caring to me before. And yes, I went to sleep thinking again, *Could this really be MY GUY?* And an answer filled my head: *YES!*

We fell in love slowly, over months of just talking and revealing ourselves bit by bit. After years of drama and pain, MY GUY finally showed up when I least expected it. Joey makes me smile, thinks about our future, and his calm demeanor helps ground the anxiety and depression I still live with. Today, I am stronger, more focused, more positive, and kinder because of him. I love and respect him, and he is an amazing father. I'll never forget the day I returned from Cielo's birth, walking off the plane in L.A. and seeing Joey's eyes filled with tears. Never in my wildest dreams did I think I'd ever find someone to share this amazing fatherhood journey with, but he couldn't wait to embrace it with me. And the day he officially adopted Cielo is one of my warmest memories.

A few years later, Joey, Cielo, and I were in Hawai'i. She and I had a surprise for Joey. I had arranged a helicopter flight over the Big Island's volcanoes, gorgeous cliffs, and waterfalls. You see, we were going to propose to Joey as the chopper flew over the most stunning of these waterfalls. Cielo, just three years old at the time, had been practicing her part over and over. Unfortunately, gloomy weather and high winds scuttled *this* wedding planner's plans. I had to quickly think of a Plan B as we were driving away from the helicopter pad. I pulled over and asked Joey to run into a little place and grab us some coffee. By the time he got back, I'd decided to drive down to this beautiful little lagoon. Cielo was on pins and needles, so ready for her lines, and kept asking, "Now, Daddy?"

"Not yet, sweetie." Inwardly I was half expecting her to pop the question from the back seat because she was so excited! I hurried as much as I safely could to get to the beach before her little heart just burst. We finally reached the destination and walked down the path to stand by the lapping surf. I got down on one knee and Cielo knew her cue.

"Tatus, will you marry us?" Cielo asked him so sweetly. (Tatus is Polish for Daddy, and Joey is Polish.)

Joey cried and said yes. It was more perfect than my first plan, because it's really hard to do a group hug in a helicopter! And so, that's how the three of us started our journey as a family. Then three years after we got married in an historic Hollywood church that had recently been restored, we welcomed our daughter Gracie—all three of us—into our lives. She has brought more love and light into our little family.

So never give up on finding your special person, just maybe don't try so hard, because I learned that when the time is right, the stars will align and you will meet the one you're destined for. I spent so many years looking so hard for my guy, and when I stopped trying, Joey showed up ready, he showed up loving, and he showed up as just himself. He lets me float when I need to, but he is always there to anchor me and to remind me what is real and worth loving. For years, I was trying to change my life, and now I wouldn't change a thing. I have a wonderful husband, two beautiful and loving daughters, and the family I always dreamed of. I have never said this to Joey, but I realize that he was an angel that brought me the safety, calmness, and love that I was missing in my heart, soul, and mind.

Simon has done that for me

CHAPTER 14

I Say Asparagus!

"**F**irst comes love, then comes marriage. Then comes baby in a baby carriage!"

Well, let me tell you, there are a few more steps in there for gay parents. Same-sex parents who choose to have children have to work very hard to bring them into the world. No "oops" pregnancies for us. In fact, similar to straight parents struggling with infertility, these are definitely babies who were planned for, and then some. To be blunt, all the parts needed to make a baby just aren't there for two men or two women.

Because Joey and I wished for our children to be biologically ours, science had to step in. Joey and I believe adopting a child is a beautiful and loving thing to do, and we may grow our family by adoption sometime in the future, but we chose to have our daughters Cielo and Gracie via surrogacy. When any child is born, it's remarkable—but it feels even more remarkable for same-sex parents. This doesn't mean our children are more special than ones conceived naturally, just that the time, coordination, money and work involved having our children makes their births feel like a true miracle. I decided to include this chapter because I've come to realize how few people really understand the word surrogacy, let alone the process of surrogacy, from start to finish. Let me break this down as simply as possible and have some fun with it at the same time, because while the journey is challenging, it's also beautiful and amazing.

So here is the cliff notes version of the Surrogacy journey:

It starts with that burning desire to be a parent and making the commit-ment to be a GREAT parent. Make sure that both future parents are fully on board for this journey and deeply wish to have a family together. This should be true for any pregnancy, of course, but given the intensity and many moving parts of the surrogacy process, this is even more important.

Typically, an agency serves like something of a matchmaker. They will find the potential partners you'll need to create the team of people that will bring your child to life.

You'll need a lawyer to handle the various in-depth contracts and agree-ments that are required—with the agency, the carrier, the egg donor, and the doctors. It is overwhelming, trust me.

Find a fertility doctor you feel comfortable with. Recommendations from other parents are the best way to do this. Your doctor is at the center of the process—the glue that literally brings all the pieces of the puzzle together.

It's time to find the first of *two* women who will play vital roles in your jour-ney to parenthood: the carrier and the egg donor. A woman can only be considered by an agency to be a gestational carrier if her current family is already complete, meaning neither she nor her husband wish for any more children of their own. The agency then sets up meetings with couples–with both the wife AND the husband—that feel totally like blind dates! The point is to ask any questions you may have and to hear why this couple wants to help others have children. Bottom line is you want to ensure they are really doing this for the right reasons.

Among the questions asked: Why do you want to do this? Have you done this before for someone else? Are you both on board and fully support this decision? How do *your* children feel about you doing this? You ask questions about their home life, their health, previous pregnancies (easy? hard? C-section?), the carrier's diet (both before and what she expects to eat during the pregnancy), and so much more. A therapist from the agency is present during this meeting, acting on behalf of both parties and helping to make things feel less awkward. He or she will also raise questions that may not have been asked or answered. Normally, when looking to find a surrogate, you'll need to meet with several couples until you feel in your gut and heart that they are the right ones to be part of this journey. Once you've decided, it's time for your lawyer to draft a detailed contract between you and your partner and the carrier and her husband.

Well, with two dads you know what we have plenty of (ahem). But without the eggs, nothing is possible. This step is about finding the egg donor. The agency provides a list of candidates, their photos, medical and psychiatric background checks, and their entire family's medical history. You also want to know everything you can about the health of the donor's parents, grandparents, and siblings. The potential donor shares her hobbies, education, career and fun facts about herself, as well as photos of her as a child and up till her current age. You can opt to meet the donor or stay anonymous. Once you choose a donor, it's back to your lawyer for yet another contract. This is a very complicated part of the process and one that requires careful consideration. We requested numerous videos of the donor to answer questions and to help us see her personality and style and energy.

Well, this is awkward, but collecting the goods is the next step. (I know you know what I mean.) Now we have the two main ingredients for our future "bun in the oven." And this is where the fertility doctor takes over. First step is the "transfer," when the doctor combines the sperm and the eggs. (You can use several eggs.)

After a few days, you find out if there are any viable fertilized eggs. Sometimes none take, and you have to go through the process all over again, which can be many months later. This step is the hardest part as it takes patience and can be very nerve-wracking. But once THE call comes that there are one or two or even three viable eggs to transfer, it's off to the doctor's office. In one small room is the carrier and her husband, the doctor and nurse, and, of course, two parents-to-be and the vial that will transfer the fertilized egg into the carrier.

Another waiting game begins as you wait to see if the fertilized egg is growing, signifying the baby-making process has begun. It can take many times for success, but you keep trying and you keep praying, and you know it will happen when it's meant to be.

It was a journey for both our daughters, some tears, worry along with excitement lead us to the two most important dates in our lives - June 19th and January 24th—the birthdays of our two girls, who are five years apart. Welcome to the world! They are kind, loving, brilliant, funny, and sweet. Cielo and Gracie arrived into the world through the modern science of surrogacy, for which we are forever grateful!

We tell the girls what each letter of their names stand for:

C – Caring	G - Grateful
I - Important	R - Resilient
E - Extra Special	A - Amazing
L - Loving	C - Courageous
O - Outstanding	I - Important
	E - Exceptional

The wake up call we have had being parents surprised us that it was not challenges with our children, rather the judgments and perceptions of two dads raising two girls. WOW, there are a lot of ignorant and insensitive people in the world, and they seem to think it's their right to comment on others' lives. "Two gay dads raising two girls?! They don't have a clue what they are doing—those poor girls!" They may think their whispers are faint, but trust me we hear and feel all of it. Over time we got used to it and learned to ignore it, but it is the abject ignorance that still stuns us the most.

Families come in all flavors: the traditional mom and dad raising children, or a single parent raising a family, or children being raised by their grandparents and/or relatives. Then there are the amazing foster parents who step up and step in to help children in need of a home. Families are beautiful and unique and special, no matter how they are formed. The idea of two moms or two dads raising children is becoming a new normal, whether some like it or not. Unfortunately, we have had more experiences than we care to remember with people who are uncomfortable with the idea of two gay parents. It's funny to me because I see some sets of straight parents and I think to myself, *Oh shit! These two can't get themselves out of a wet paper bag. I worry for their kids!*

It has been an eye-opening experience raising our two girls as two dads. (We hated being called "the two gays" but are so happy to now be called "the two dads!" Ironic, I know.) Our little family is often stared at as if we are aliens from Mars just dropped down to Earth. (I'd like to drop a *house* on some of these witches and remind them that we can tap our gay ruby red shoes far better than they can!) Joey and I have experienced countless times when a stranger asks us where the mother is—as if it's anyone's business! Or a flight attendant will ask our girls as we are disembarking a plane, "Where is your mom? Or even worse they have said…. "is she dead?"

Are you freaking kidding me? This literally happened. If a female friend joins us when we are out with the girls, strangers will immediately assume she is the mother of our girls. The real kicker is that often our female friends are far too old to even *be* our girls' mom. Initially, when we heard remarks like this, we avoided confrontation because our focus is on our girls and not the ignorant person asking insulting questions. Finally, we both realized it would be nice to share our story. A simple reply we use is "This is our friend, and these are *our* two daughters, and our friend is not their mom."

We live in such a myopic culture that if something isn't as a person believes it "should" be, then it must be wrong or bad or disgusting. Now more than ever in our current, polarizing political and social climate, anyone of a different race or religion who doesn't align with someone's mindset is either judged, called names, or worse. People give unsolicited opinions (usually loudly), or simply a nasty look, or the whispering behind us—it's all so petty and mean. My feeling is they should mind their own damned business! African-Americans have been judged by white people for decades, just as Jews have been persecuted for centuries, and Asians are now being blamed for things that have absolutely nothing to do with them.

It's sad and a disgrace when people can't see the beauty and the love of all people. The ones slinging insults are the ones who need to look a bit closer and longer in the mirror. I would suspect that no matter how long they stare in the mirror, they will see the same thing we see when looking at them: anger, judgment, and an unwillingness to accept change or see that *love* is *love*, and that it lives within all of us. Anyone *can* make a shift and change if they want, but the bigger question is: Will they? I am not looking to change the world, but I am looking to shine some light on the beauty of *all* families. Hell, even my own father does not acknowledge my daughters as his grandchildren. My mom loves them both so, so much, and she and Cielo have a very special connection. She now has advancing Alzheimer's disease (I'll share more about that in the next chapter), and so she didn't really get a chance to develop a relationship with Gracie, but she always smiles and laughs when she sees our youngest.

Joey and I are adults, with thick skin, and we knew we'd face scrutiny and judgment when we decided to have a family. But when our daughters are the target, back the hell off. You've heard of mama bears protecting their young? Well, papa bears can be just as fierce. We were so fortunate when Cielo started Pre-School at a wonderful, loving school with accepting and open-minded staff and parents. I think we were the first gay family to enroll, so they actually went above and beyond to make us all feel comfortable and we did. In fact, we were stunned by their love and kindness. This school asked us what we'd like to do for their Mother's Day celebration, and we said we didn't need to be there since we're her dads! But the Father's Day party was so special with both of us there. There was the time they wanted to get photos of the kids with all of the moms for one shot, and with all of the dads for another. The director told Joey and I to join both photos! I laughed and said, "See, it pays to be gay since we get two pictures for the price of one!"

I guess we got a little spoiled at that school and unwittingly set expectations of tolerance and acceptance that weren't as universal as we'd hoped. When we moved to a different area just outside of L.A., we enrolled Cielo at a new school. Cielo came home and told us that her classmates kept telling her that she was adopted – or that her mother was dead…this was everyday! And one mean child was just relentless, which is shocking given that the kids were in Pre-K! How in the hell would children that young learn such intolerance? From their parents of course. I wrote a letter to the school's director, copying the child's parents and the class teacher as well. Of course the first person we heard from was not the Pre School, rather it was the bullies father. The bully's father falsely accused me of calling him homophobic in the letter I wrote to make him and his wife aware of their child's behavior. He approached me in the parking lot at pick-up time a few days later, puffing out his chest and trying to start something *in front of the kids!* Joey was standing there with me, and this guy said, "I'm not homophobic! I have a gay assistant!"

It was laughable, really and while Joey and I could handle his stupidity and use it to show our daughter how to stand up, be proud and share her story. The preschool, did acknowledge our letter, but not surprisingly, their apathy towards it reminded me of *my* middle school and high school days when no one did a thing to help me with Mr. English. Well, that sure as hell wasn't going to happen to my daughter.

This experience really made us think about where to send Cielo to elementary school, public vs. private. We enrolled her in a well-known private school it had all the bells and whistles, including ballet, music, theater, science, technology, and more. Joey and I were impressed and felt that it was worth the steep tuition and would be a wonderful place for Cielo. We naturally assumed things would be different there. How wrong we were. Cielo started coming home sad and in tears, because *again* she was being taunted that she was adopted since she had two Dads. We brought the headmaster and Cielo's teacher three sweet, easy books to explain surrogacy. We even offered to come in on read-aloud day to share the books with the class so they would understand Cielo's family better. But they declined, saying the books were not in their curriculum . . . and again nothing was done. In fact, it only got worse.

Cielo told us that one of her classmates hit her repeatedly with a metal water bottle. We complained to the administration but to no avail. Mornings became hell since she did everything possible to avoid going to school. But the day we got the phone call that this same classmate came up behind Cielo and cut off four inches of her hair was the last straw. We flew down to the school to bring her home. Cielo's classmate did apologize to her, saying, "she cut her hair out of anger she had at her father". God knows what was going on in that family but clearly this child was acting out and none of the staff were doing anything about it. Cielo shared other information as well, which we included in a letter to the headmaster and staff to document the behavior this student directed at our daughter. While we were told our concerns were being taken seriously, given their previous inaction, we didn't expect anything to change. Needless to say, we pulled Cielo out of that school.

As parents, we send our children off to school each day assuming that their classmates, teachers, administrators, and other parents teach these young people that life is beautiful and that everyone deserves to feel respected-that all forms of families are unique. We expect they will be given the tools to be the best version of themselves, and to listen and learn and gain confidence to step forward in life with a perspective that they can help others, bring joy, and lift the spirits of others. Joey and I work hard to lead with positivity because positivity is powerful!

To my dismay, I realized not much had changed from the days when I was bullied for being different. And that makes me profoundly sad. . . sad for our girls and for all children. Parents have to find the right environment for their children, knowing they are respected and understood so they can grow with love, confidence, and strength.

So we changed schools *again* and finally found a wonderful, accepting school that brought a smile back to our daughter's face and has rekindled excitement for learning and life.

We had explained to Cielo as best we could, given her age, how she came into this world and into our hearts. She was so cute and kept asking us every day before going off to her new school, "What is that word again?"

"Surrogacy," we said.

All she wanted was to be able to share this knowledge with her classmates. Each morning driving her to school, I'd hear her in her car seat whispering to herself. At first I couldn't really hear what she was saying, thinking it might just be a little song or poem she was saying to herself. Then, after a few weeks, I heard her say over and over, in her sweet little voice, "Asparagus, asparagus, asparagus."

Surprised, I asked her if she liked that vegetable.

"Daddy," she replied, "I am wanting to make sure to say it right, so my friends know how I came into the world through asparagus."

I smiled and was so proud of her. Now every time I walk through the produce section of the grocery store, I smile when I pass the asparagus, reminding myself to keep teaching my girls that all families are unique and special.

You say surrogacy, I say asparagus—either way you say it, it means family.

CHAPTER 15

My Best Friend

My father was sitting across from my brother and me at the Garden Restaurant in Port Chester, uncharacteristically quiet and nervous, fiddling with his silverware but not eating a bite. My brother, a quiet man on a good day, was even more stoic than usual. And this was *not* a good day. Our father's affair with a local woman had come to light—and my mother's world had come crashing down. Everybody's business is everybody's business in a place like Port Chester, and the entire town was already aware of what had happened.

His marriage, his reputation, his ego—everything was now on the line . . . and he wanted me and my brother to help fix things! Maybe because we were adults in our twenties at the time, he had some twisted notion that he could talk to us man-to-man? Explain why he did what he did and help him smooth things over? Fuck that! I didn't give a damn about his "explanation." This was our mother, our devastated and humiliated mother, who had borne the brunt of his selfishness.

I had never disrespected my parents. Ever. Even when my father would not accept me as gay, I swallowed his insulting comments and opinions and just walked away. But this was about my mom. I laid into him so hard it shocked even me. Told him he had no right to try to put his children in the middle of this mess he had created and that he had to fix this shit show on his own. I left there furious and heartbroken—furious at him and heartbroken for my mother.

My mom leaned on me for support, and all I wished was that I could just rewind time and make it so that it had never happened. And as filled with rage as I was with my father for trying to use me to help him mend things, I just couldn't be angry when my mom looked right at me and asked, "What should I do? Should I still love your father?"

Should she leave him or stay? The woman I knew, so full of fun and life, was utterly destroyed. I'll never forget that moment—the moment when I felt like I had failed my mother. In my head I thought, *Leave him . . . . allow yourself to be free and to be the person you want to be and not the person he sees you as or wants you to be.* But I didn't tell her to leave because I could see how painful that would be for her as well. They were high school sweethearts. You meet, you like someone, you love them and take them for who they are, you marry, and you raise kids. 'Til death do us part. She still believed in that. And I still can't help but wonder what she would have done for herself—what she could have become if I'd been stronger for her then.

My regret at not telling her to leave and start a new life over thirty years ago comes back to haunt me daily now. My dear, sweet, big-hearted mother is receding into Alzheimer's—a cruel disease that is stealing her personality, memories, and life, day by day. And my father, of course, is in charge of her care, or in my mind, the lack thereof. Now, she is steadily declining under his watch. At first, she would just be in the same spot at home all day or—how's this for history repeating itself?—he would take her with him in the hearse when he had to go out for work! I absolutely realize that in my mom's cognitive state, she doesn't know a hearse from an airplane, but what upsets me is that there are better options. She needs to be in an environment of calmness, peace, grace, and love—and I have researched and found wonderful memory-care facilities designed specifically for people suffering from Alzheimer's.

On the rare occasions my father will accept my phone calls, his response is always the same: "I have it under control. I know what I am doing and

I have a plan." God forbid, he should ever admit he could use help or ever ask for it. Instead he actively rejects it, and my mother suffers for it.

My frustration turned to fury when I was in Jamaica for work in the fall of 2021, and my aunt (my mother's much younger sister) phoned me to let me know that my mom had fallen at home, resulting in a broken nose, contusion on her forehead, and two black eyes. Worse yet, my family waited four days—four freaking days!—to take her to the hospital. Beside myself (and thank God Joey was with me to calm me down), I was ready to drop everything and fly to New York. But first I made the dreaded call to my father, who pretty much shrugged it off and wondered why I was so upset.

"She fell," he said, stating the obvious. "Just slipped and fell." And then as if reading from the same script I've heard him recite my entire life: "I have it under control."

The call ended as most calls with my father have since I stopped taking his shit years ago. Me raging at him that he may CONTROL everything and everyone, but he has never had anything UNDER control. And then he hangs up on me.

It has been difficult being an entire continent away from my mother and being denied even just the chance to hear her voice on the phone because my father forbids it or my brother won't pass along a message to her. The process to actually speak to my mom requires that I text my brother, who, in turn, texts me back and will say anything from "call in five hours" or "call right now, not five minutes later." My brother, having lived under my father's roof his entire life, does what he's told. I know that ultimately it's my father calling the shots. When I do finally succeed in getting my mom on the phone, I only have a minute or so to talk with her.

A few years ago, when I was on the east coast with my oldest daughter Cielo and wanted to visit my mom, my father actually *took her out of the house* beforehand to make sure I wouldn't be able to. Cielo was understandably upset because she adores Grammy. It's like he has decided to hold my mother hostage from me—as well as my daughter. As her husband, he *does* legally control everything regarding her, so it's not as if he is threatened by me and my efforts (futile though they are) to try to improve her remaining days. Does he think I'm going to swoop in and kidnap her? Believe me, the thought has crossed my mind. But even taking his domineering and controlling nature into consideration, he is doling out a cruel punishment that I will never understand.

I never in a million years thought that I'd have to work so hard just to speak to my own mother. Picking up the phone and calling my mom was something I used to do regularly every morning. Just a quick hi and catch up. Or sometimes a bit more, depending upon what was going on. We would talk about the great, the good, and sometimes not-so-good moments in my life. She was then—and still is—my inner voice, which makes up in small part for the fact that she can no longer articulate her insight, direction, advice, and ideas. But she imparted so much strength and warmth and wisdom over the years, and I still have many messages on my phone from Mom that I saved since 2014, when I was beginning to realize that the calls were getting shorter and her ability to connect with me in our conversations was becoming a bit harder. I cherish these recordings.

Many nights, especially these days, I go back and listen to those messages to just hear her voice. Just to remind myself of her energy. Though soft-spoken, I can imagine her smile and the sparkle in her eyes when I replay the messages. Her voice always made her sound so young. She always made a point to make sure I was feeling the very best before we said goodbye. Our calls always ended something like this: "Mom, I love you" and, not wanting the call to end, she would say, "I love you." Pause. And then again, "I LOVE you." Pause. Then perhaps a little giggle. "Love you. OK." Pause. "Don't forget I LOVE you!" Then, I would then chime in and say "LOVE you, Mom."

What I realize now is we both were stalling to avoid having to hang up.

•• ● ● ● ••

I may not have advised my mom to leave all those years ago, but I did my best to see that she enjoyed life to the fullest. Because *she* had always made sure I was able to live life to the fullest. (And nothing ever seemed to bother her. I recall driving around with her in her little red Dodge Dart. It was a convertible, so even more awesome to me as a kid. She didn't even mind when it started to rain; we just kept on driving and laughing!)

My mother is and always was the light of and the light *in* my life. She said, "*You can do this!*" when others didn't think my dreams were possible. She was the staunchest ally for my fledgling business and career, and after it was off the ground and flying, she worked with me for the better part of sixteen years. She had been working as a nurse's assistant at one of the local schools and told me she wasn't being treated well.

"So why not come and work for me?" I asked.

She said "yes," without a second thought and began a period full of the fondest and most wonderful memories of my life and, I like to think, hers.

I'm not saying this because she is my mom, but she was literally an amazing employee. My entire staff loved her, and she was the glue the held us all together—she was the office mom to us all. And we never fought! As my personal assistant, she kept my schedule straight, booked all my travel, and also answered calls from potential clients. Clients and vendors and absolutely everyone we worked with loved JoAnn Corsaro. We made sure that she used her maiden name professionally, and I believe that increased her confidence. I made a point of calling her JoAnn at work but often slipped up and called her Mom.

Because her very first job was at General Motors, she was a master of shorthand. She would write everything first in shorthand (when did they stop teaching that in school? It's such an amazing, useful skill!) and then transcribe her notes for us.

One of the best things was bringing Mom to the set of my TV show. She'd walk around and chat with the crew and marvel at how it all came together. A huge perk during the time my mom worked with me: she was always invited to the Kennedy Center Gala that I produced for many years. She met Tony Bennett and felt like a queen for a day!

Mom supported me, accepted me without question for whomever I was turning out to be—both in my professional and in my personal life—and, most of all, she *believed* in me. She was so proud of my accomplishments. As the years went by and my business expanded and more opportunities presented themselves, she was always there to share in my successes and, more importantly, get me through the hard times as well.

One thing my mother always dreamed of doing was traveling. Whenever she brought it up to my father, however, it was "*No!* Not interested!" He has always been completely happy to stay in his hometown bubble, which meant my mother stayed there as well. Being stuck in Port Chester, in a house with my father who knew only about Port Chester, her world was limited. Traveling the world seemed like an impossible dream. But after I had some success under my belt and the means to help make my mother's dreams a reality, it was full speed ahead!

One day we sneaked out, and she got her first passport so we could go anywhere. (Needless to say, my father was none too happy it, but he did let her go—I'll give him that.) It became my mission to show her the world. This was well before the onset of her Alzheimer's, and I thank God she was able to appreciate every single moment, every single memory.

Traveling with my mother was such a gift to me and for her. We took off for Rome, Venice, Tuscany, Sienna, Monte Carlo, Paris, Quebec City, among other wonderful places. We also explored great cities here in the States. Santa Fe was a particular favorite; in fact, she ended up redecorating her living room in desert designs and colors after one trip. There was an outdoor opera there that she adored, plus we took hikes through the beautiful desert, ate amazing food, and, of course, shopped!

Mom never once said no when I suggested a destination, and I am convinced she always had a bag packed in advance (hidden under the bed?), ready to go whenever and wherever I suggested a trip. She loved to shop and look at art and take in museums. I believe that even though she decided to stay in her marriage, something fundamental shifted inside her at the same time, and she was finally determined to make herself happy. I swear to God she was another person when she was away from Port Chester, or should I say, she transformed into the woman she truly was inside. She loved learning, loved exploring, and loved being in the moment.

Upon seeing the little villages around Rome and Tuscany for the first time, she was moved to tears by the beauty and soul of these old towns. On our second trip to Italy, we went to Venice, where she was in seventh heaven. My favorite souvenir from our travels was from this particular trip. We took a water taxi to Murano Island, famous for its centuries-old tradition of glassmaking, and together designed a stunning chandelier for the New York City apartment I was moving into upon our return. All these years later, it now hangs in the California home I share with Joey and our daughters. It's one of my most treasured items—mostly for the warm memories it conjures every time I look at it. Unfortunately, we never did get to Calabria, which is where my maternal grandfather was from. Or Umbria, in the north, from where Nana's family hailed. Pop-Pop, the dark southern Italian, and Nana, the fair-haired, fair-skinned northern Italian, made such a pair. My daughter Cielo inherited my grandmother's beautiful complexion and hair.

On another trip, we spirited away to Paris the week before Christmas. It was beyond wonderful. A gorgeous city any time of year, it was magical then. We walked and walked and shopped and shopped. Despite having grown up on Italian food in predominantly Italian Port Chester, my mother has a pretty daring palate. She tried things I wouldn't touch if you paid me— pigeon, rabbit, venison, foie gras. (Food is *not* a place where I explore my adventurous side!) But she wanted to experience it all. I'll never forget the morning we headed up to Montmartre, where the artists and their works

line the streets. Aside from what seemed like miles of paintings and draw-
ings, the artists were singing Christmas carols, and Mom just melted, crying and smiling in equal measure.

New York City had been my base of operations for my businesses and TV
shows for years, which meant it was easy for me to see my mother regularly.
But after I had been filming *My Fair Wedding* for four years, the network
called and offered me a new season with many episodes and said, "David,
you pick the city you want to shoot the show in . . . NYC, Dallas, or Los
Angeles."

I didn't event take a breath before I said, "Los Angeles."

My mother was my biggest cheerleader for that decision, even though it
would take me as far as possible from my East Coast home—and her--
without getting my feet wet. The timing was right to move to L.A., and she
never tried to hold me back, even though we knew we'd miss each other
tremendously. I moved into a hotel that first year, then rented a home in
Brentwood, and eventually moved to another rental in Bel Air. I absolutely
loved California. My life had changed dramatically and for the better. Yet
I found that while 3,000 miles apart is a lot, it still wasn't far enough to
completely erase the pain and sadness, nor fix all that was wrong with my
family relationships. And I worried about leaving my mother behind.

After I relocated, I invited my mother for extended visits—typically every
three to four months for several weeks at a time—and I swear her whole
being improved while she was here. The trips refreshed and healed my
mom from the stress and drama that was going on back home. I scheduled massages, acupunture, and chiropractor visits. We walked miles on
the beach. We went to movies, to great restaurants, to parties at friends'
houses, and we even threw parties at our home for Mom's birthday.

She happened to be visiting over Halloween once and dressed up as the
Wicked Witch of the East to our Tin Man, Scarecrow, Dorothy, and Toto.
I am certain Mom inherited her sense of adventure and fun from her

mother, my dear Nana. Mom would try anything! She would jump on an ATV with me in the rain and fly through puddles of mud. She would don a life preserver and go rafting in Class IV rapids. Space Mountain in Disney World did give her a run for her money, however. She got so dizzy she had to rest, but rallied and was ready to keep going a few hours later.

Mom was also the person who found my little doggie. It was on one of her first trips to L.A. when one morning she saw this dirty, skinny little dog in our yard and brought it inside. I took one look at her and said, "Hello, Lucy! I Love *you* Lucy!" (My infatuation for Lucille Ball surely played a huge role in that moment.) So, Lucy became a part of our family that day (and just in time to play Toto on Halloween!), thanks to my mom. And Lucy was so much more to me. She was my constant companion when I was traveling all over the country doing my TV show. She flew with me, stayed in my hotel room with me, and gave me a sense of home and love when I'd come back after a long day on the set.

What's really special about my life with Lucy is up to that time, I was terrified of dogs. Yes, even little dogs. It all started when I was a boy. I used to walk to school every single day from kindergarten to sixth grade—and every single day, BJ, a white-and-brown mixed breed, would chase me when I'd walk by his house. I'd cross the street to avoid him, and it didn't matter. He sensed my arrival and probably smelled my fear. He never did catch me or bite me, but the anxiety of walking past that house, anticipating the attack that never came, was almost as bad as if he had bitten me.

When I was older, I had a newspaper route. One of my deliveries was to a house with a tiny black dachschund. What he lacked in size, he made up for in moxie. *That* one actually did catch me, biting my ankle as I tried to speed away on my bike. Once I gave up the paper route, I started mowing lawns. At one house, this large, menacing German shepherd, tied to his dog house by a rope, always barked and lunged at me. At least he couldn't reach me— until the day he broke his rope, raced across the lawn, and attacked me. His owners came out and pulled him off of me. (Why didn't they just keep him inside while I was mowing, I'll never know.) And that was the final straw for me and dogs, until sweet little Lucy came into my life. Even as an adult when I dated Michael, a professional dog handler, I never accompanied him to any dog shows.

When my mother found Lucy and brought her into my house, I'm sure she had no idea how profoundly Lucy would impact my life. Lucy became the child I didn't yet have, and I swear taking care of her prepared me in so many ways for becoming a parent. And Lucy was a part of that, too! When I got the call that my daughter Cielo was about to be born via a surrogate, Lucy and I flew to Kansas to await her arrival. The nurses at the hospital were simply wonderful and would go to the hotel to feed and walk Lucy since I was spending every moment with my newborn, who was born early and had to spend a month in an incubator. And every night, I would bring one of her blankets back to the hotel so Lucy could get familiar with her scent. On the day I finally got to bring my Cielo home, one of the nurses picked Lucy up at the hotel and took her to her own home. I met them there and set the car seat with my tiny bundle on the front lawn, so they could be properly introduced. I swear Lucy *knew* that was *her* baby, too!

Aside from visiting me regularly in L.A., my mother and I spent years making up for lost time, doing anything and everything that would allow her to feel peaceful, happy, and relaxed. My father was put out that I took her away so often and so far, but I didn't care—and I am pretty sure, finally, she didn't either! For me it was the best gift—I had my Mom, all to myself. I remember hating when she had to leave, in large part, knowing she'd be heading back to that suffocating, controlling environment.

That move to California gave me space—literally and figuratively—to help me accept that while I couldn't change the family that I was born into, I *could* emotionally detach from them since they didn't love and respect me. So that is exactly what I did—I stepped away and I made sure to arm myself with love from other people who accept me for who I am. It's not as easy as I thought it would be, and I still struggle with the disconnection from my family to this day. We have to protect our hearts, our minds, and our lives, and we must do that however we can. It took me a long time, but I finally figured out that courage is caring for yourself first, and then the well is full for you to care for others. I have dealt with anxiety and fear for years; it never completely goes away, but it does not have to mean failure. Everyone struggles. God knows I have. But when you realize that struggles can be turned into success, it becomes the turning point in your life.

Was it the Southern California sun, the more laid-back surroundings, or simply being away from all the nonsense back home in New York that led me to this growth and acceptance? I'm guessing it was a combination of all three, as well as just finally coming into my own and feeling confident. Yet there is a lingering helplessness that the long distance from my mom has brought on, especially as her disease has progressed. I can't imagine life without her, yet I'm in limbo to help her the way she needs me to.

After a time, my mother's trips to L.A. became more challenging since my father didn't want her travel to the West Coast alone. The very beginnings of what would eventually be diagnosed as Alzheimer's were starting to show—some disorientation, memory issues, and anxiety when she traveled by herself. So, I would fly to New York City, meet Mom, and fly back with her to California. After our time together, I'd fly home with her and then turn right around and head back to L.A. It was always sad to say goodbye, but we talked and planned visits knowing we'd see each other again soon. I loved our shared times in L.A. Those extended visits were the best gift for my soul.

As the years passed and her Alzheimer's disease began to advance, the trips stopped, and our time together became less and less. And once my father was in control again, I knew my ability to see here would be curtailed. But I knew I needed to be in L.A., and she knew that, too, and we made the most of her trips west while she was able to enjoy them.

Beyond that, I am so incredibly grateful for the abundance of quality time I got to spend with my mom as an adult: working together for over a decade, traveling internationally, our times at my house in Connecticut, and then those fabulous weeks in California.

Life is all about finding the time, making it happen, and having wonderful memories to take away from those moments, no matter how brief. I *know* the soul of my mom is still somewhere within her, even though Alzheimer's conceals this from the outside. When I talk to her, I tell her I'm her son David who loves her. I hope that gentle reminder of who I am sparks something in the recesses of her mind that will let her remember even a little something about me. I conclude my short phone calls by always saying "thank you" to my mom—thank you for making me who I am. Reminding her to always keep smiling, I finish with letting her know that I am the person I have become today because of her and her love for and acceptance of everyone. She pauses and I hear her breathe and I ask, "Are you okay?" and she says, "Yes!" and then she says thank you and tells me just how much she loves me. It's a moment in time, but each of these short moments for me is golden.

This precious time with my mother brings to mind something I just can't understand: Why do people disappear? Friends of hers she has known for decades seemingly have vanished. Perhaps they couldn't deal with what was happening to their dear friend JoAnn? Or they didn't want to be a part of it because they were scared it might be them next? While my mother may not remember everyone's names or their memories together, she recognizes the sound of love and caring, be it over the phone or in person. Harsh as it sounds, I call those who have disappeared from her life cowards, and each and every one of them should be ashamed of their lack of action.

Not long ago, there was a phone call different from all the rest. While they all are challenging now and tinged with sadness, this call was different. My mother has a hard time putting words together to make complete sentences, so I always do my very best to keep our conversations short. Like many people with Alzheimer's, she doesn't remember names. But on this call she said, "I have to see you and Cielo." It was lucid, it was direct, she remembered Cielo's name, and I knew that was a big deal. And I knew we had to go. She never asks for anything, but she asked for this.

I looked at dates, and Joey booked our flights and hotel, and Cielo and I were off to see Grammy. The connection always has been strong between Grammy and Cielo. I was riddled with anxiety, but I knew I had to head to the East Coast to see my mom. Immediately.

It's always hard for me to go back to the house where I grew up. But my mother was the best part of it during my childhood and still is today. Yet my anxiety was high on that flight back to New York. I wasn't prepared to see a situation that was not going to show the best version of my mom and that alone was more than I thought I could handle. Cielo picked up on my nerves back in L.A. and on the flight. For someone so young, my oldest daughter is very aware of her surroundings and picks up on the energy of others and tries to move it toward the positive, if possible. Cielo held my hand and was even more loving than normal as we landed at JFK.

After getting settled in our hotel in Greenwich, Connecticut, we got in the rental car to go visit my mother, Cielo's Grammy. I took a deep breath as we pulled up in front of the house. My emotions were in overdrive. How does one feel both excitement and dread in the same moment? Happiness and sadness in the same breath? Everything about this trip felt polarizing. Pick an emotion—I was feeling it.

Mom was sitting in the far corner of the sofa in the living room, just staring straight ahead. The house is small so you can't miss anyone walking into the room. When she saw us, she started to cry. She also had a smile, yet she didn't say anything. What surprised me the most was her appearance. My mom loved to dress up, wear jewelry, and have her makeup and hair done. But there she was with messy clothing, her hair almost fully white, no makeup, and shoes that were ripped and dirty and that looked uncomfortable. I sat by her side and held her hand, speaking softly to her and telling her my name and Cielo's, and I realized fully and with deep sadness that the woman she used to be was no longer there.

My father was sitting at the dining room table, quiet when we first arrived, but then he got up and proceeded to leave, saying he was off to the funeral home to work. No details, no instructions of what to do if Mom needed something, no word on when he would be returning. He turned his control knob to the passive-aggressive setting. I know it was his way of trying to show just how badly he had it. It didn't matter because I knew what he would say—the same things he'd said to me over the last two years whenever I got him to answer my calls. He'd rant about all the frustrating and unpleasant aspects about caring for my mother in her deteriorating state, always telling me how terrible he had it, and what he had to put up with. Caring for a person with Alzheimer's is one of the most brutal and difficult things a spouse can ever have to do. I understand that completely. But when I'd remind him that there were wonderful care facilities or even in-home help available, he'd have none of it. How could he continue the role of martyr if he actually accepted help? I knew he was trying to guilt trip me and, of course, I felt bad. But what was worse was his tone of voice and the unloving way in which he spoke of her; she couldn't take care of any more herself, and so he had to do all of these things for her.

After my father left that day, Cielo went over and sat by her Grammy, taking out her iPad and showing her various games and such. I had to step away for a phone call, and when I returned to the room, Cielo was showing my mother how to play one of her games! There was my mom, changing the colors on the screen, drawing lines, and totally engaged! She was smiling and had an entirely different look on her face than what I saw when we first arrived. Rather than letting her just sit in the corner alone, Cielo went into my mother's world and managed to draw her out, if just for a while. People with this cruel disease are trapped inside their bodies and minds and often look hollow, lost, and simply not present. They may smile and cover up memory loss the way that people do who know they're forgetting things—apologies, some nervous laughter at their forgetfulness, or maybe pretending to remember. They seem to know that they *don't* know. But right then, in that moment with her granddaughter, my mom was *present*.

Cielo sensed what both her Grammy *and* I needed. As a parent, you never want to burden your child with your emotional struggles, but she saw my sadness and did what she could to lighten the energy in the house. We turned off the TV, which was just white noise left on all day long, and Cielo put on music and started to dance. And my mother loved it, smiling and almost looking like the woman she had always been.

On the second day of our trip, my father left us alone again to head to work, and again with no helpful information. It was like he wanted to say, "Here, *you* see what it's like to live with her now."

I was actually grateful for the time alone with my mother and daughter—and I did indeed notice how helpless my mom had become. She had an accident, and so together Cielo and I slowly led her up the stairs to the bathroom. My mom can barely walk, so getting her up the short flight of stairs was no easy feat. I held onto Mom, and Cielo started to sing a counting song as we took one step at a time. We tried to make a fun game of it. And it worked. But what Cielo did not see was my fear and the tears rolling down my face. I got Mom into the small bathroom and asked Cielo to stay outside to sing and tell jokes so she would not have to be a part of what I needed to do.

I removed my mom's clothes and her soiled diaper and then proceeded to clean her up. But there was nothing to work with: no wipes, no clean adult diapers. She had a hard time lowering herself down to sit on the toilet and an even harder time getting up.

Later, I asked my father to please have the needed items in the bathroom to help me take care of Mom. But when it happened again the next day, there was still nothing there. I am fully convinced he wanted me to suffer and do what he does every day, all day. And I *do* appreciate how hard it is, and I would do anything for my mother—but the point is there is help available. My nana had an aide in her house, then went to an assisted living home where she could get the help and support she needed. I *know* from the days I spent helping my mother that it is a hard and heartbreaking job. And despite the fractious relationship I have with my father, I know the toll it is taking on him as well. But it doesn't have to be that way.

• • ● ● ● • •

None of us knows how long we have with the people we love. I know that my time with my beloved mother is getting shorter, and it breaks my heart. Some may think it's premature or even a bit maudlin to give a eulogy for someone before they've passed, but there is so much I want to say to honor my mother, and I already have those words in my heart, so I am sharing them here because I want everyone—not just those who will be present to say goodbye to my mother—to know what an amazing woman the world will be losing.

I have been stuck in darkness and sadness over the course of these past years, with such mixed feelings, yet hoping that it would be sooner rather than later to give my mom the peace she deserves.

Alzheimer's showed up very early time in Mom's life (just sixty-seven years of age when the first signs emerged). She was too young. She was not ready, and she did not deserve it, though no one is ever ready or deserves to be stricken with any disease.

When I needed advice, or comfort, or just a voice . . . I could call Mom, and she was always there to offer simple insights on what to do and how to handle each moment. As the Alzheimer's advanced, my calls with my mom started to become shorter and shorter . . . but I held on to each and every word she spoke. Thirty-minute calls became fifteen minutes, then ten minutes, then shrunk to five minutes, and then they would only last sixty to ninety seconds, at the most. But what I loved the most was when I asked her how she was doing, and she would reply, "Everything is great!" She never complained and she never wanted me to worry, even when I knew things were not going well.

The woman didn't have a bad bone in her body. My mom. My best friend. My coworker. My cheerleader. Our children's Grammy. She lived a life of joy . . . a life of love . . . a life of acceptance . . . a life of kindness . . . a life of peace and happiness. She was a woman that simply loved to smile!

JoAnn Corsaro-Tutera was not just a mom, a sister, a wife, a friend. My mom was someone who deeply cared about everyone. And she loved to create lists! These lists allowed for her to make sure that she was seeing everyone that she loved and adored. She had a List 1 and List 2 (though neither one was more important than the other). List 1 contained the names of people whom she had not seen; List 2 was who she had just seen. It was how she made sure she saw everyone and never missed a moment. She called everyone just to check in and had a list a mile long for birthday cards and gifts to be sent.

From kindergarten through marriages and the arrival of children and grand-children, my mother shared a remarkable bond with three lovely ladies: Carole Fulco, Ro Clarke (my godmother), and Marianne Pergamo, her dearest lifelong friends. We should all be so lucky to find the love and devotion these four women had over the course of their lives together. I honor all of them!

Everything good, kind, and caring about me comes from my mom. She exuded kindness and acceptance of all and saw only beauty and love in others. For me she was my cheerleader, always saying to me, "You can do this . . . I believe in you." She accepted me for being gay, welcomed our daughters with no questions—only pure love!

Mom was always ready for anything and never held back. She wanted to see what was beyond the walls of Port Chester. I am grateful for the abundance of time we shared and the trips we took together. One of my favorite photos that I keep in my bedroom is of the two of us in the middle of St. Mark's Square in Venice, feeding the pigeons at sunrise. Just the two of us together, just being there, just creating that memory.

Mom, thank you for being you, for adding love, positivity, and pure joy to this world. This moment is not goodbye; this moment is a reminder of who you are and the bright light you brought into this world that was often dark. Your bright light will forever shine in me and others. I love you . . . and I am lucky that you are my mom standing by my side!"

EPILOGUE

've been asked many times why I've added so many tattoos to my body. I have a sleeve of ink on my right arm, my left hand, on the right side of my chest, and over my right shoulder, as well as on the left side of my back. And I'm not done yet.

My body art reminds me every single day of the challenges I've faced and survived—and the joy that has emerged over the years. We can't just pretend that some of the worst times in our lives will simply disappear. Many of us try to forget or attempt to bury the pain. But that only works for so long, and then we are forced to face our past. Everything we do, every experience becomes a part of who we are, how we think, and what we choose to do—or not do—in our future.

The butterflies on my body are for change; the flowers are for rebirth, as in the rebirth of love and living when life has pushed us down. We have options, and we can bloom into whoever we wish to be.

My hope was that in sharing my story, I could help others see we are never alone. Everyone is struggling with something. But there is always a way through the dark; there is always someone you can reach out to for encouragement, or for help, or just to hear your story. At the end of this book is a list of resources that can point you in the right direction. And I also hope you had a few laughs reading this as well—I know I did recalling some of the stories.

Enjoy the journey and always dream big.

David

RESOURCES

We all need guidance and support at times in our lives. Here are some not-for-profit organizations that I wish had been in *my* life when I was growing up.

Rachel's Challenge

Rachel's Challenge addresses the root causes of school violence, bullying, prejudice, and self-harm through social-emotional learning programs that build connection, hope, and resilience. This organization works to improve school culture, so that students are able to reach their full potential academically, socially, and emotionally. rachelschallenge.org/

To Write Love On Her Arms

To Write Love on Her Arms is a nonprofit movement dedicated to providing hope and finding help for people struggling with depression, addiction, self-injury, and suicide. The organization exists to encourage, inform, inspire, and invest directly into treatment and recovery. twloha.com/

The Trevor Project

The Trevor Project is the world's largest suicide prevention and mental health organization for lesbian, gay, bisexual, transgender, queer & questioning (LGBTQ) young people. Offering a suite of 24/7 crisis intervention and suicide prevention programs. Trevor also operates an education program with resources for youth-serving adults and organizations as well as a research team to discover the most effective means to help young LGBTQ people in crisis and end suicide. https://www.thetrevorproject.org/

Born This Way Foundation

Born This Way Foundation, cofounded and led by Lady Gaga and her mother, Cynthia Germanotta, supports the mental health of young people and works with them to build a kinder and braver world. Through high-impact programming, youth-led conversations, and strategic cross-sectoral partnerships, the foundation aims to make kindness cool, validate the emotions of young people, and eliminate the stigma surrounding mental health.

https://www.bornthisway.foundation

ACKNOWLEDGMENTS

The light that shines onto my heart and soul allows me to step forward every day with grace and love. The journey I have lived and the joy I have experienced far outweigh the heartache, sadness, and challenges.

To say I am blessed with love is an understatement. I am forever grateful for the encouragement and love from my mom. She saw me, she heard me, and she loved me just as I am with no judgment and with no questions. Thank you, Mom, for always reminding me that "you can do this." I am stronger and bolder in each step I take because of you. You will always and forever be in my heart, and I am part of you as you are of me. We made a great team, and together we enjoyed so many moments in life. You loved to laugh, you loved to shop, and you loved to love others. Mom, you will forever and always be my best friend!

I am forever grateful for the three wonderful people that make up *my* family! Joey—my husband, my partner in life, and my biggest supporter—I love you deeply. You know how to push me when it is needed; you are there for me when I fall, and you pick up the pieces. You are a ray of light and love for me and for our girls. Anyone who has the opportunity to be in your light will be forever changed by it. I look forward to all that we will do together as husband and husband and as parents to our two beautiful and sweet and loving daughters. We are a true partnership . . . and you are "My Guy," and thank God we found one another. I look forward to raising our sweet, silly, smart, and loving girls together.

Cielo and Gracie . . . you both have changed my life for the better. Your love for life and playfulness in each day propels me into a place of sheer happiness. I look forward to every day, hour, and minute with you both. To say I am blessed is simply a cliché. To say I am happy and feel loved and protected is more accurate. Thank you, Cielo and Gracie, for bringing pure joy into my heart and allowing me to see life through your eyes. You have opened my eyes up to a clearer vision of life from the perspective of the two of you.

Projects don't just happen and come to fruition without a lot of hard work and time. When I decided to bring my story to life, I knew I needed some very special and very talented people who knew me . . . really knew me and knew my life and where I came from. This journey of sharing my life was not the easiest for me emotionally, but I knew that if my story could shed some hope, some life, and some love onto others, it would be worth it. Bette Kennedy and Chuck Fulco took my words, my stories, my tears, and my joy from my life and together stitched it into something beautiful, which is this book. Your dedication, love for details, and concern of my feelings and my heart has meant so much to me. It always takes a team to work closely together. These past two years of writing together has truly been an honor and a joy. I will forever be grateful to you both.

Costco

- gravy
- pies
- Brie
- crackers
- Hummus
- apples
- pears
- almonds
- Salami
- Parmesan (grated)
- green beans
- rolls
- beer
- wine

Ralphs / T.J's

- Orzo
- spinach
- Olive oil
- garlic
- Salt / pepper
- butter
- jam
- salad
- manchego
- pecans
- apples ?
- pears ?
- whip cream

Thanksgiving 2023

- gravy > Costco
- pies > Costco > apple, pumpkin, berry?
- green beans - parmesean, garlic, olive oil
- Orzo salad - double n triple?
- Rolls > Costo
    - butter / jam
- Brie > Costco
    crackers
    pears / apples / almonds
    Hummus?
    Salami
- whip cream > buy
- green salad w/ apples, mandrango, pecans
    apple cider vinegar dressing

Annette - potatoes
         cranberries

Mr. Trezise - turkey
              stuffing